Lessons in Project Management

Tom Mochal and Jeff Mochal

Apress®

Lessons in Project Management
Copyright ©2003 by Tom Mochal and Jeff Mochal

Technical Reviewer: Clive Gilson

Editorial Board: Dan Appleman, Craig Berry, Gary Cornell, Tony Davis, Steven Rycroft, Julian Skinner, Martin Streicher, Jim Sumser, Karen Watterson, Gavin Wray, John Zukowski

Assistant Publisher: Grace Wong

Copy Editor: Ami Knox

Production Manager: Kari Brooks

Compositor: Kinetic Publishing Services, LLC

Proofreader: Lori Bring

Interior and Cover Designer: Kurt Krames

Manufacturing Manager: Tom Debolski

Library of Congress Cataloging-in-Publication Data

Mochal, Tom, 1957–
   Lessons in project management / Tom Mochal and Jeff Mochal.
      p. cm.
   ISBN 1-59059-127-5
   1. Project management.   I. Mochal, Jeff, 1974–   II. Title.
   HD69.P75M626 2003
   658.4'04—dc22   2003015831

Printed and bound in the United States of America 10987654321

Distributed to the book trade in the United States by Springer-Verlag New York, Inc., 175 Fifth Avenue, New York, NY, 10010 and outside the United States by Springer-Verlag GmbH & Co. KG, Tiergartenstr. 17, 69112 Heidelberg, Germany.

In the United States: phone 1-800-SPRINGER, email orders@springer-ny.com, or visit http://www.springer-ny.com. Outside the United States: fax +49 6221 345229, email orders@springer.de, or visit http://www.springer.de.

For information on translations, please contact Apress directly at 2560 Ninth Street, Suite 219, Berkeley, CA 94710. Phone 510-549-5930, fax 510-549-5939, email info@apress.com, or visit http://www.apress.com.

This book is dedicated to my wife, Pam, and my children, Lindsay, Sean, and Ashley. Without their love, support, and good humor, none of my work would be possible.

—Tom Mochal

To my beautiful wife, Erika, who inspires me everyday to be a better man and a better husband. Thank you for your constant support and unconditional love. And to my brother and coauthor, Tom, for the opportunity to create a fictional world in which he could dispense some very brilliant project management advice.

—Jeff Mochal

Contents by Story

1 Jerry Doesn't Realize He Is Managing a Project 9

2 Ashley and the Disappearing Sponsor 13

3 Mike's Client Has Status Report Envy 17

4 Lindsay Finds Activities Are Always 90 Percent Complete 21

5 Susan's Small Enhancement Has Grown into a Project 25

6 Jerry Starts to See the Light 28

7 Poor Reyna—Trapped in Workplan Minutia 31

8 Jerry Learns Firsthand the Need to Manage Documents 35

9 Danielle Takes Scope Definition to Heart 38

10 Patrick Discovers the Three "Best Friends" of Project Managers . . . 41

11 Jerry's Project Takes a Turn for the Worse—Maybe 45

12 Time for Tom to Take Some of His Own Medicine 48

13 Miles Learns an Important Lesson—for the Second Time! 51

14 There's a Problem, but No One Tells Mike 55

15 Ashley Is About to Gain an Hour a Week 59

16 Jade Resolves a Vendor Problem (Again and Again) 63

17 Bailey Has Questions, but She Is Not Sure What They Are 67

18 The Project Nobody Wants 71

19 Jade Discovers a "Baby" Risk on Her Project 74

20 Jerry Has a Small Problem (Unfortunately in Front of the CIO) 77

21 I'm Eating a Burrito, Jeff's Eating His Contingency 80

22 Communication Is King on Reyna's Project 83

23 Ron, the New Guy, Learns About Project Management Scalability . . 86

24 Brian Can't Plan First, but He Still Needs to Plan 89

25 Ashley Finds Not All Critical Path Activities Are "Critical" 92

26 Jerry Is Told to "Sharpen His Pencil" to Reduce an Estimate 96

27 Jean Needs to Add a Personal Touch 101

28 Erika's Quality Plan Needs More Quality 104

29   Sean Is Losing the Deadline Battle—a Little at a Time 107

30   Jerry Jumps into the Workplan Too Quickly 110

31   Danielle Is Sensing Risky Business 114

32   Mike Receives a Change Request He Needs to "Scope" Out 117

33   Chucky May Be Crazy About Collecting Metrics 120

34   Alex Has 200 Projects to Estimate! 123

35   Sean Makes a Guess and I Make a Prediction 127

36   Lindsay Wishes for a Problem-Solving Magic Wand 130

37   Terri and Sarah Propose Half-Measures 134

38   John Is the "Risk Eliminator," but Does He Need to Be? 137

39   Nikki and Her Client Have Mismatched Expectations 140

40   Alex's Project Is in Good Shape—Maybe 143

41   Sean "Errors" by Not Managing Quality Early 147

42   Danielle Has Satisfied All Her Clients—Except One 150

43   Lindsay Has a Halloween Fright—
     Her Project Is Behind Schedule 153

44   Marty Has a Work Breakdown 158

45   Rick Thinks Our Status Reports Taste Like Stale Fish 162

46   It's Magic! Lauren Sees an Assumption Turn into an Issue 166

47   Sally May Be Squandering Her Good Fortune 170

48   Marc Finds the Work Slipping When Everyone Is Responsible 174

49   Lauren Needs to Complete a Never-Ending Project 177

50   Heather Finds Her Facts Don't Win Any Points 180

Contents by Lesson

1 Understand the Characteristics of a Project 10

2 Make Sure You Always Have an Identified and Committed
Sponsor and Client Organization 14

3 Report Status on All Projects (There Are Many Alternatives
to the Format and Delivery) 18

4 Focus on Deadline Dates First When Managing a Project 23

5 Apply Some Level of Project Management Discipline—
Even on Small Projects 26

6 Define and Plan the Work First to Ensure Better
Project Execution 30

7 Don't "Microbuild" or Micromanage the Workplan 32

8 Manage Documents Properly to Avoid Confusion
and Mix-Ups 36

9 Define the Many Aspects of What Is in Scope
and out of Scope 39

10 Use the "Big Three" Documents—Project Definition,
Project Workplan, and Requirements—As the Foundation
for Your Project 42

11 Use Scope Change Management to Allow the Sponsor
to Make the Final Decision (Many Times the Sponsor
Will Say "No") 46

12 Collect Metrics to Evaluate How Well You (and Your Project)
Are Performing 49

13 Save Knowledge for Future Projects, Leverage Knowledge
from Prior Projects 52

14 Ensure Issues Management Is Everyone's Responsibility 56

15 Shorten Long Meetings to Sharpen the Focus 60

16 Identify the Root Cause of Problems, Especially If They
Are Reoccurring 64

17 Use Quality Assurance Techniques to Validate
the Status of a Project 68

18   Cancel Projects That Lose Business Support,
     Relevance, and Focus 72

19   Use Risk Management to Respond to Problems
     Before They Occur 75

20   Focus Your Quality Management on Processes,
     Not People 78

21   Don't Use Your Estimating Contingency for
     Scope Changes 81

22   Develop a Communication Plan to Address
     Complex Communication Requirements 84

23   Scale Your Project Management Processes Based
     on the Size of the Project 87

24   Define and Plan the Project, Even If You Have to
     Start the Work at the Same Time 90

25   Understand the Critical Path on Your Project and
     How This Path Drives the Deadline Date 93

26   Change the Underlying Assumptions to Revise a
     Well-Prepared Estimate 97

27   Don't Shortchange Face-to-Face Communication
     on Your Project 102

28   Make Sure Quality Is a Mindset and an Ongoing Process
     on Your Project 105

29   Batch Small Scope Change Requests Together
     for Sponsor Approval 108

30   Define the Overall Project Approach Before Building
     the Detailed Workplan 111

31   Look for Risks Inherent to Your Project Before You Begin 115

32   Get Sponsor Approval Before Investigating Large
     Scope Change Requests 118

33   Make Sure the Cost of Collecting Metrics Does Not
     Exceed Their Value 121

34   Use One or More Formal Techniques to Estimate
     Project Work Effort 124

35   Keep Your Workplan Up to Date Throughout the Project 128

36   Use Issues Management to Help Choose the Best
     of Bad Alternatives 131

37   Collect Metrics That Can Lead to Fundamental
     Improvements 135

38   Evaluate All Risk Response Options in the Risk Plan 138

39   Gain a Common Understanding First to Effectively
     Manage Client Expectations 141

40   Use Milestones in the Workplan to Track Overall Progress 144

41   Establish Processes to Catch Errors As Early in the
     Project As Possible 148

42   Gain Sponsor Approval for Scope Changes Requiring
     Budget and Deadline Changes 151

43   Be Proactive in Applying Techniques to Accelerate
     the Project Schedule 154

44   Use the Work Breakdown Structure Technique to Identify
     All the Work Required for a Project 159

45   Write Your Status Reports with the Readers'
     Interest in Mind 163

46   Update Your Risk Plan Periodically Throughout
     the Project 167

47   Don't Practice Goldplating—Delivering More Than
     the Client Requested 171

48   Make Sure One Person Is Responsible for Each Activity
     in the Workplan 175

49   Focus on Your Deadline Date to Keep Your Project
     from Wandering 178

50   Collect Metrics, but Gain Agreement on Their Significance
     Ahead of Time 181

Story and Lesson Chronology

Story #	Timeline	Title	Lesson(s)	Character
1	January 4	Jerry Doesn't Realize He Is Managing a Project	Understand the Characteristics of a Project	Jerry Ackerman
2	January 5	Ashley and the Disappearing Sponsor	Make Sure You Always Have an Identified and Committed Sponsor and Client Organization	Ashley Parker
3	January 13	Mike's Client Has Status Report Envy	Report Status on All Projects (There Are Many Alternatives to the Format and Delivery)	Mike Miller
4	January 15	Lindsay Finds Activities Are Always 90 Percent Complete	Focus on Deadline Dates First When Managing a Project	Lindsay Peterson
5	January 20	Susan's Small Enhancement Has Grown into a Project	Apply Some Level of Project Management Discipline—Even on Small Projects	Susan Chang
6	January 27	Jerry Starts to See the Light	Define and Plan the Work First to Ensure Better Project Execution	Jerry Ackerman
7	Early February	Poor Reyna—Trapped in Workplan Minutia	Don't "Microbuild" or Micromanage the Workplan	Reyna Andersen
8	February 7	Jerry Learns Firsthand the Need to Manage Documents	Manage Documents Properly to Avoid Confusion and Mix-Ups	Jerry Ackerman
9	February 14	Danielle Takes Scope Definition to Heart	Define the Many Aspects of What Is in Scope and out of Scope	Danielle Bartlett
10	Mid-February	Patrick Discovers the Three "Best Friends" of Project Managers	Use the "Big Three" Documents—Project Definition, Project Workplan, and Requirements—As the Foundation for Your Project	Patrick Henley

Story #	Timeline	Title	Lesson(s)	Character
11	February 22	Jerry's Project Takes a Turn for the Worse—Maybe	Use Scope Change Management to Allow the Sponsor to Make the Final Decision (Many Times the Sponsor Will Say "No")	Jerry Ackerman
12	End of February	Time for Tom to Take Some of His Own Medicine	Collect Metrics to Evaluate How Well You (and Your Project) Are Performing	Tom (me)
13	End of February	Miles Learns an Important Lesson—for the Second Time!	Save Knowledge for Future Projects, Leverage Knowledge from Prior Projects	Miles O'Brien
14	First Monday of March	There's a Problem, but No One Tells Mike	Ensure Issues Management Is Everyone's Responsibility	Mike Miller
15	March	Ashley Is About to Gain an Hour a Week	Shorten Long Meetings to Sharpen the Focus	Ashley Parker
16	March	Jade Resolves a Vendor Problem (Again and Again)	Identify the Root Cause of Problems, Especially If They Are Reoccurring	Jade Johnson
17	First week in April	Bailey Has Questions, but She Is Not Sure What They Are	Use Quality Assurance Techniques to Validate the Status of a Project	Bailey Jenkins
18	Mid-April	The Project Nobody Wants	Cancel Projects That Lose Business Support, Relevance, and Focus	Emma Flood, Curtis Chapman, Jennifer Adams
19	April 30	Jade Discovers a "Baby" Risk on Her Project	Use Risk Management to Respond to Problems Before They Occur	Jade Johnson
20	May 1	Jerry Has a Small Problem—Unfortunately in Front of the CIO	Focus Your Quality Management on Processes, Not People	Jerry Ackerman
21	May 5	I'm Eating a Burrito, Jeff's Eating His Contingency	Don't Use Your Estimating Contingency for Scope Changes	Jeff Erickson
22	May 5	Communication Is King on Reyna's Project	Develop a Communication Plan to Address Complex Communication Requirements	Reyna Andersen

Story #	Timeline	Title	Lesson(s)	Character
23	May 28	Ron, the New Guy, Learns About Project Management Scalability	Scale Your Project Management Processes Based on the Size of the Project	Ron Klinger
24	June	Brian Can't Plan First, but He Still Needs to Plan	Define and Plan the Project, Even If You Have to Start the Work at the Same Time	Brian White
25	June	Ashley Finds Not All Critical Path Activities Are "Critical"	Understand the Critical Path on Your Project and How This Path Drives the Deadline Date	Ashley Parker
26	End of June	Jerry Is Told to "Sharpen His Pencil" to Reduce an Estimate	Change the Underlying Assumptions to Revise a Well-Prepared Estimate	Jerry Ackerman
27	July 1	Jean Needs to Add a Personal Touch	Don't Shortchange Face-to-Face Communication on Your Project	Jean Combs
28	July 3	Erika's Quality Plan Needs More Quality	Make Sure Quality Is a Mindset and an Ongoing Process on Your Project	Erika Thompson
29	July	Sean Is Losing the Deadline Battle—a Little at a Time	Batch Small Scope Change Requests Together for Sponsor Approval	Sean Robinson
30	July	Jerry Jumps into the Workplan Too Quickly	Define the Overall Project Approach Before Building the Detailed Workplan	Jerry Ackerman
31	Last week in July	Danielle Is Sensing Risky Business	Look for Risks Inherent to Your Project Before You Begin	Danielle Bartlett
32	August	Mike Receives a Change Request He Needs to "Scope" Out	Get Sponsor Approval Before Investigating Large Scope Change Requests	Mike Miller

Story #	Timeline	Title	Lesson(s)	Character
33	August	Chucky May Be Crazy About Collecting Metrics	Make Sure the Cost of Collecting Metrics Does Not Exceed Their Value	Charles Riley
34	August	Alex Has 200 Projects to Estimate!	Use One or More Formal Techniques to Estimate Project Work Effort	Alex Jordan
35	Last week of August	Sean Makes a Guess and I Make a Prediction	Keep Your Workplan Up to Date Throughout the Project	Sean Robinson
36	September	Lindsay Wishes for a Problem-Solving Magic Wand	Use Issues Management to Help Choose the Best of Bad Alternatives	Lindsay Peterson
37	September	Terri and Sarah Propose Half-Measures	Collect Metrics That Can Lead to Fundamental Improvements	Terri Milner, Sarah York
38	Third week of September	John Is the "Risk Eliminator," but Does He Need to Be?	Evaluate All Risk Response Options in the Risk Plan	John Santos
39	Last week of September	Nikki and Her Client Have Mismatched Expectations	Gain a Common Understanding First to Effectively Manage Client Expectations	Nikki Hooper
40	First week of October	Alex's Project Is in Good Shape—Maybe	Use Milestones in the Workplan to Track Overall Progress	Alex Jordan
41	Second week of October	Sean "Errors" by Not Managing Quality Early	Establish Processes to Catch Errors As Early in the Project As Possible	Sean Robinson
42	October	Danielle Has Satisfied All Her Clients—Except One	Gain Sponsor Approval for Scope Changes Requiring Budget and Deadline Changes	Danielle Bartlett
43	October 31	Lindsay Has a Halloween Fright—Her Project Is Behind Schedule	Be Proactive in Applying Techniques to Accelerate the Project Schedule	Lindsay Peterson

Story #	Timeline	Title	Lesson(s)	Character
44	November 1	Marty Has a Work Breakdown	Use the Work Breakdown Structure Technique to Identify All the Work Required for a Project	Marty McKnight
45	November, week of Thanksgiving	Rick Thinks Our Status Reports Taste Like Stale Fish	Write Your Status Reports with the Readers' Interest in Mind	Rick Goodall
46	November	It's Magic! Lauren Sees an Assumption Turn into an Issue	Update Your Risk Plan Periodically Throughout the Project	Lauren Carter
47	Late November	Sally May Be Squandering Her Good Fortune	Don't Practice Goldplating— Delivering More Than the Client Requested	Sally White
48	December	Marc Finds the Work Slipping When Everyone Is Responsible	Make Sure One Person Is Responsible for Each Activity in the Workplan	Marc Reynolds
49	December, week before Christmas	Lauren Needs to Complete a Never-Ending Project	Focus on Your Deadline Date to Keep Your Project from Wandering	Lauren Carter
50	December, last day of the year	Heather Finds Her Facts Don't Win Any Points	Collect Metrics, but Gain Agreement on Their Significance Ahead of Time	Heather Cruise

Cross-Reference of Project Management Processes and Lessons

Project Management Step	Story #	Title	Lesson	Character
1. Define the Work	1	Jerry Doesn't Realize He Is Managing a Project	Understand the Characteristics of a Project	Jerry Ackerman
1. Define the Work	2	Ashley and the Disappearing Sponsor	Make Sure You Always Have an Identified and Committed Sponsor and Client Organization	Ashley Parker
1. Define the Work	5	Susan's Small Enhancement Has Grown into a Project	Apply Some Level of Project Management Discipline—Even on Small Projects	Susan Chang
1. Define the Work	6	Jerry Starts to See the Light	Define and Plan the Work First to Ensure Better Project Execution	Jerry Ackerman
1. Define the Work	10	Patrick Discovers the Three "Best Friends" of Project Managers	Use the "Big Three" Documents— Project Definition, Project Workplan, and Requirements— As the Foundation for Your Project	Patrick Henley
1. Define the Work	18	The Project Nobody Wants	Cancel Projects That Lose Business Support, Relevance, and Focus	Emma Flood, Curtis Chapman, Jennifer Adams
1. Define the Work	23	Ron, the New Guy, Learns About Project Management Scalability	Scale Your Project Management Processes Based on the Size of the Project	Ron Klinger
1. Define the Work	24	Brian Can't Plan First, but He Still Needs to Plan	Define and Plan the Project, Even If You Have to Start the Work at the Same Time	Brian White

Project Management Step	Story #	Title	Lesson	Character
1. Define the Work	30	Jerry Jumps into the Workplan Too Quickly	Define the Overall Project Approach Before Building the Detailed Workplan	Jerry Ackerman
2. Build the Workplan	26	Jerry Is Told to "Sharpen His Pencil" to Reduce an Estimate	Change the Underlying Assumptions to Revise a Well-Prepared Estimate	Jerry Ackerman
2. Build the Workplan	34	Alex Has 200 Projects to Estimate!	Use One or More Formal Techniques to Estimate Project Work Effort	Alex Jordan
2. Build the Workplan	40	Alex's Project is in Good Shape—Maybe	Use Milestones in the Workplan to Track Overall Progress	Alex Jordan
2. Build the Workplan	44	Marty Has a Work Breakdown	Use the Work Breakdown Structure Technique to Identify All the Work Required for a Project	Marty McKnight
3. Manage the Workplan	4	Lindsay Finds Activities Are Always 90 Percent Complete	Focus on Deadline Dates First When Managing a Project	Lindsay Peterson
3. Manage the Workplan	7	Poor Reyna—Trapped in Workplan Minutia	Don't "Microbuild" or Micromanage the Workplan	Reyna Andersen
3. Manage the Workplan	25	Ashley Finds Not All Critical Path Activities Are "Critical"	Understand the Critical Path on Your Project and How This Path Drives the Deadline Date	Ashley Parker
3. Manage the Workplan	35	Sean Makes a Guess and I Make a Prediction	Keep Your Workplan Up to Date Throughout the Project	Sean Robinson
3. Manage the Workplan	43	Lindsay Has a Halloween Fright—Her Project Is Behind Schedule	Be Proactive in Applying Techniques to Accelerate the Project Schedule	Lindsay Peterson

Project Management Step	Story #	Title	Lesson	Character
3. Manage the Workplan	48	Marc Finds the Work Slipping When Everyone Is Responsible	Make Sure One Person Is Responsible for Each Activity in the Workplan	Marc Reynolds
3. Manage the Workplan	49	Lauren Needs to Complete a Never-Ending Project	Focus on Your Deadline Date to Keep Your Project from Wandering	Lauren Carter
4. Manage Issues	14	There's a Problem, but No One Tells Mike	Ensure Issues Management Is Everyone's Responsibility	Mike Miller
4. Manage Issues	16	Jade Resolves a Vendor Problem (Again and Again)	Identify the Root Cause of Problems, Especially If They Are Reoccurring	Jade Johnson
4. Manage Issues	36	Lindsay Wishes for a Problem-Solving Magic Wand	Use Issues Management to Help Choose the Best of Bad Alternatives	Lindsay Peterson
5. Manage Scope	9	Danielle Takes Scope Definition to Heart	Define the Many Aspects of What Is in Scope and out of Scope	Danielle Bartlett
5. Manage Scope	11	Jerry's Project Takes a Turn for the Worse—Maybe	Use Scope Change Management to Allow the Sponsor to Make the Final Decision (Many Times the Sponsor Will Say "No")	Jerry Ackerman
5. Manage Scope	21	I'm Eating a Burrito, Jeff's Eating His Contingency	Don't Use Your Estimating Contingency for Scope Changes	Jeff Erickson
5. Manage Scope	29	Sean Is Losing the Deadline Battle—a Little at a Time	Batch Small Scope Change Requests Together for Sponsor Approval	Sean Robinson

Project Management Step	Story #	Title	Lesson	Character
5. Manage Scope	32	Mike Receives a Change Request He Needs to "Scope" Out	Get Sponsor Approval Before Investigating Large Scope Change Requests	Mike Miller
5. Manage Scope	42	Danielle Has Satisfied All Her Clients—Except One	Gain Sponsor Approval for Scope Changes Requiring Budget and Deadline Changes	Danielle Bartlett
6. Manage Communication	3	Mike's Client Has Status Report Envy	Report Status on All Projects (There are Many Alternatives to the Format and Delivery)	Mike Miller
6. Manage Communication	15	Ashley Is About to Gain an Hour a Week	Shorten Long Meetings to Sharpen the Focus	Ashley Parker
6. Manage Communication	22	Communication Is King on Reyna's Project	Develop a Communication Plan to Address Complex Communication Requirements	Reyna Andersen
6. Manage Communication	27	Jean Needs to Add a Personal Touch	Don't Shortchange Face-to-Face Communication on Your Project	Jean Combs
6. Manage Communication	39	Nikki and Her Client Have Mismatched Expectations	Gain a Common Understanding First to Effectively Manage Client Expectations	Nikki Hooper
6. Manage Communication	45	Rick Thinks Our Status Reports Taste Like Stale Fish	Write Your Status Reports with the Readers' Interest in Mind	Rick Goodall
7. Manage Risk	19	Jade Discovers a "Baby" Risk on Her Project	Use Risk Management to Respond to Problems Before They Occur	Jade Johnson
7. Manage Risk	31	Danielle Is Sensing Risky Business	Look for Risks Inherent to Your Project Before You Begin	Danielle Bartlett

Project Management Step	Story #	Title	Lesson	Character
7. Manage Risk	38	John Is the "Risk Eliminator," but Does He Need to Be?	Evaluate All Risk Response Options in the Risk Plan	John Santos
7. Manage Risk	46	It's Magic! Lauren Sees an Assumption Turn into an Issue	Update Your Risk Plan Periodically Throughout the Project	Lauren Carter
8. Manage Documents	8	Jerry Learns Firsthand the Need to Manage Documents	Manage Documents Properly to Avoid Confusion and Mix-Ups	Jerry Ackerman
8. Manage Documents	13	Miles Learns an Important Lesson—for the Second Time!	Save Knowledge for Future Projects, Leverage Knowledge from Prior Projects	Miles O'Brien
9. Manage Quality	17	Bailey Has Questions, but She Is Not Sure What They Are	Use Quality Assurance Techniques to Validate the Status of a Project	Bailey Jenkins
9. Manage Quality	20	Jerry Has a Small Problem— Unfortunately in Front of the CIO	Focus Your Quality Management on Processes, Not People	Jerry Ackerman
9. Manage Quality	28	Erika's Quality Plan Needs More Quality	Make Sure Quality Is a Mindset and an Ongoing Process on Your Project	Erika Thompson
9. Manage Quality	41	Sean "Errors" by Not Managing Quality Early	Establish Processes to Catch Errors As Early in the Project As Possible	Sean Robinson
9. Manage Quality	47	Sally May Be Squandering Her Good Fortune	Don't Practice Goldplating— Delivering More Than the Client Requested	Sally White
10. Manage Metrics	12	Time for Tom to Take Some of His Own Medicine	Collect Metrics to Evaluate How Well You (and Your Project) Are Performing	Tom (me)

Project Management Step	Story #	Title	Lesson	Character
10. Manage Metrics	33	Chucky May Be Crazy About Collecting Metrics	Make Sure the Cost of Collecting Metrics Does Not Exceed Their Value	Charles Riley
10. Manage Metrics	37	Terri and Sarah Propose Half-Measures	Collect Metrics That Can Lead to Fundamental Improvements	Terri Milner, Sarah York
10. Manage Metrics	50	Heather Finds Her Facts Don't Win Any Points	Collect Metrics, but Gain Agreement on Their Significance Ahead of Time	Heather Cruise

About the Authors

Tom Mochal has over 23 years of IT experience and is currently president of TenStep, Inc., a project management and methodology consulting and training company. Tom has published hundreds of columns, and has presented and trained on project management and life-cycle topics around the world. He has developed a complete project management methodology called TenStep (http://www.tenstep.com), a methodology for implementing and supporting project management within companies called PMOStep (http://www.pmostep.com), and a methodology to help companies implement portfolio management (http://www.portfoliostep.com). Tom's prior experience included positions at Eastman Kodak, Cap Gemini E&Y, The Coca-Cola Company, and Geac Computers.

Jeff Mochal has been working in the public relations/marketing, advertising, and communications industries for the last five years. He is an experienced writer, editor, and communications strategist who has worked for several clients in fields such as sports, technology, fast food, and public affairs. He also has several years of experience in crisis communication, field marketing, event planning, and product publicity. Jeff has worked for International Management Group (IMG), Rogers & Associates, Brener Zwikel & Associates, and currently works in St. Louis for Jordan Associates.

About the Technical Reviewer

Clive Gilson is a freelance technical editor who has some 20 years of practical experience in the IT industry. Clive has worked at a senior level for some of the world's leading IT service providers in both operational and project management capacities. He has recently taken up full-time editing and writing for a range of publishers and publications.

Introduction

This book represents my 24 years of experience working on projects, managing projects, and managing people who were managing projects. Like most project managers when they start out, I did not sit down and learn project management before I started managing projects. Initially, managing projects just meant determining what needed to be done and then working with one or more people to get it done. After managing projects a few times, I become more comfortable planning out the work and managing it to completion. These projects ranged from small and large enhancement projects to multimillion dollar initiatives.

This type of project management is typical of the way most people manage projects today. Most project managers have very little formal project management training, and no mentoring at all. They do, however, have good organizational skills and a good feel for the work needed to complete the deliverables required for the project. If they are really good, they also have decent estimating skills, which will ensure they have enough budget and time to complete the project.

That was my story until the mid-1990s, when I was a director at a large beverage company. When I took the position, I inherited a number of projects—one of which was politically sensitive and under pressure to complete within a 6-month deadline. The approach of the previous project manager seemed reasonable enough; however, it ultimately became clear the work involved with the project was greatly underestimated. For a variety of reasons, the project took almost 18 months to go live—not the 6 months originally estimated.

From my perspective, the most frustrating part was not being able to provide the guidance and coaching needed for the project, which was one of a number of competing priorities. More importantly, however, I felt I did not have the formal project management knowledge required to rescue it. I tried to provide coaching, and at one point set up daily meetings with the project manager, but it seemed a case of the blind leading the blind. As a result, this project went down as the only initiative to fail on my watch.

My next assignment at the same company was to build a Project Management Office (PMO) and deploy formal project management processes throughout the worldwide IT organization. I started as the manager of the methodology support team and gradually acquired more responsibility until I became the program manager of the entire initiative.

This allowed me to make the transition from the typical "seat-of-your-pants" project manager to one who understood the methodology side as well. When your job is to build the methodology and then coach and train others, you gain an in-depth understanding of project management and how to do it well. So, that is what I did for three years.

Fortunately, my team and I had a solid foundation to start with. We did not build a methodology from scratch. Instead, we utilized an existing methodology from a Big-5 consulting firm as our starting point, and then customized the processes for our purposes. Still, we did a ton of work to build the specific processes, templates, best practices, training classes, etc., needed by our organization. As we were building content, we were also coaching and training the worldwide staff. It was a very busy and challenging three years.

Although our methodology was a good one, I could sense that managers and team members were frustrated when they applied it to their specific projects. First, like many commercially available project management methodologies, there was way too much material to absorb. The content associated with the methodology took up many, many manuals. These were not 20-page manuals either—some were 500 or more pages long! Granted, some of the content was repeated when applied to differing types of projects, but the reason the manuals were so large was the methodology. It was developed to manage the largest, most complex projects imaginable.

Of course, no one expected our project managers to utilize the entire process. The objective was always to pick and choose the portions that made sense for their particular project. One of the jobs of our PMO was to go through the methodology and customize the material in a manner easier for people to get their heads around. However, it was difficult to scale the process down appropriately. Subsequently, most managers felt they were applying more project management time and effort than was required. I found out quickly that if project managers feel like the project management methodology provides value, they tend to use it. On the other hand, if they think the process is more cumbersome than necessary, they resist changing how they manage their projects.

When I left after three years, I thought a lot about what I had learned. I spent most of my career managing work without formal project management training. Now I had formal training and experience using a mega-methodology, but I knew there was something better. I wanted to apply my background and experience to create a process that project managers would understand and accept. The result is the TenStep Project Management Process(r) (TenStep) available at `http://www.tenstep.com` (TenStep is described in more detail in "Background: The TenStep Project Management Process").

When I developed TenStep, I focused on two overriding principles. First, the methodology would be scalable, meaning it would be easy to understand and apply for project managers managing small, medium, and large projects. This allows project managers to manage small projects with a minimum level of project management structure and not feel guilty. It also applies a much higher level of project management structure to large projects without apology.

Second, the 10 steps of the TenStep methodology would be aligned in a way that represents a progression of project management competencies. The lower steps represent processes every project manager should practice on every project. As the steps get higher, more rigor and sophistication are typically required, especially for larger and more complex efforts.

As I mentioned previously, in addition to building project management methodology, I also had the pleasure of coaching and training project managers around the world. As I was doing this coaching, I realized it was easier for project managers to learn if I included examples within the lessons. For instance, it was easier for project managers to learn scope change management if I could apply the principle to their projects, including specific examples of applying scope change management, as well as examples about misusing the process. If I could not think of examples relevant to specific projects, I would come up with examples from other projects they could relate to.

This book is the culmination of that teaching method. The marketplace is full of project management books, columns, best practices, tips, and traps. The question is not, Can you find project management content? The question is, Will you remember it at the appropriate time to apply it on your project?

Let's face it—very few columns or books are compelling enough to be read over and over again. That is the case with project management content. Project management books tend to get read once (or maybe just scanned) and never picked up again. I felt I could communicate a project management lesson more effectively if I could tell a story, a parable perhaps, that showcases a project management lesson. As the reader, you would have the context of how the lesson really applies on a project. The lesson would then be easier to understand and, more importantly, to remember.

This book applies 50 important project management lessons in 50 easy-to-digest stories. In addition to the main lesson, each story also mixes in other project management concepts and definitions the reader can absorb as well. The book also comes with a great follow-up reference Web site for further project management information—http://www.tenstep.com.

I hope you find the information in this book valuable in your job, and I hope you can apply the lessons to your projects.

Once again, read. . . remember. . . apply.

Background: The TenStep Project Management Process

Project management refers to the definition, planning, and subsequent management, control, and conclusion of a project. All projects need some level of management. The larger and more complex the project, the greater the need for a formal, standard, and structured process. Smaller projects still need a structured process, but the process does not need to be as elaborate or as complex. Obviously, there is a cost to the effort associated with project management, but many benefits are obtained as well, and the benefits far outweigh the costs.

The TenStep Project Management Process(tm) (TenStep) is designed to provide the information you need to be a successful project manager, including a step-by-step approach, starting with the basics and getting as sophisticated as you need for your particular project. TenStep is a flexible, scalable methodology for managing work as a project. The basic philosophy is "large methodology for large projects, small methodology for small projects.(tm)" TenStep shows you how to manage projects of all sizes.

ABOUT THE TENSTEP NAME

The TenStep "steps" represent a need for more and more project management discipline and control as your project gets larger and larger. For example, all projects should be defined (step 1), even if you do not have a workplan. Of course, as projects get bigger, a workplan is needed as well (step 2). If you create a workplan, you need to manage it (step 3). No matter how small your project is, when problems arise, you need to resolve them (step 4). As a project gets larger, you need to worry about scope change (step 5), etc.

The bottom line is a small project rarely has formal quality plans, and they rarely include a metrics process. From a scalability perspective, they don't need to. However, when you are dealing with larger and larger (longer and longer) projects, you reach a point where all of the steps are important. Project managers should be planning (steps 1 and 2) and managing (steps 3 through 10) all aspects of large projects in parallel. However, smaller projects will focus on fewer project management processes.

1

Not surprisingly, the TenStep Project Management Process is segmented into 10 steps—the first two for definition and planning, and the next eight for managing and controlling the work. The following pages provide a high-level overview of the TenStep process and the purpose of each step.

STEP 1 DEFINE THE WORK

Before project work begins, time must be spent planning the work. In this step, the project manager defines the work to ensure the project team and customers have a common understanding of the project. This includes defining and agreeing upon what is going to be delivered and when, what it will cost, who will do the work and how it will be done, and what the benefits will be. The larger the project, the more important it is for these factors to be mapped out formally and explicitly.

All projects should start with this type of up-front planning to prevent future problems caused by differing viewpoints on the basic terms of the project. The major deliverable from this step is the Project Definition (some companies call this a charter*).*

STEP 2 BUILD THE WORKPLAN

In this step, the project workplan is created. The workplan is a vital tool to ensure the project team knows what it needs to do. Different approaches should be taken in this step according to the size of the project. The workplan for small projects can be built without a lot of formality. It is possible to use a project management package like MS Project, a spreadsheet, or a piece of paper. The project manager can sit down with other team members, if appropriate, and lay out the work to be performed.

If you do not have a workplan template to use as your starting point, the work breakdown structure (WBS) technique can be used for both medium and large projects. TenStep discusses the steps to creating a workplan from scratch, starting with a WBS, sequencing the activities, adding dependencies to create a network diagram, adding effort hours, resources, etc.

STEP 3 **MANAGE THE WORKPLAN**

You have created a Project Definition and a project workplan. Now you must manage the workplan and ensure it represents the current status of the project. The workplan should be kept up to date and should always tell how much work is remaining.

For the most part, the workplan will need to be reviewed on a weekly basis. During this review, it should be updated to show work completed. It is also important to identify work not yet completed, as well as work that should have been completed but isn't. The remaining work should be evaluated to see if the project will be completed within the original effort, cost, and duration. The workplan can be further adjusted according to this information.

Other factors to consider when determining project progress include a comparison of budget and actual expenditures made, any signs the project may be in trouble, and an examination of the project's critical path. There are a number of techniques to utilize if your project is behind schedule or is projected to go over budget.

For any size project, the first priority should be to complete the project within the original estimates for effort, duration, and cost. If any of the original estimates cannot be met, new estimates need to be prepared and communicated to your management and to the customer. Future work should be replanned on a monthly basis to reflect any additional information or detail.

STEP 4 **MANAGE ISSUES**

If a problem arises that the project manager and team can resolve, then it is just one of the many fires put out in a given week. However, an "issue" arises when a problem will impede the progress of the project and cannot be resolved by the project manager and project team without outside help. This step provides guidance on putting a process in place to ensure the appropriate people are aware of the issue and can resolve it as quickly as possible. There are also a number of problem-solving techniques identified to help resolve these issues.

Issues management is one of the fundamental processes of TenStep, and it is a skill all project managers must master. Most projects have issues arise. Once an issue has been identified and possible consequences have been investigated, it must be resolved quickly and effectively. Issues cannot be ignored, and they cannot be deferred to some later time. Appropriate stakeholders need to be informed of any changes to the original Project Definition caused by the issue and its resolution.

STEP 5 MANAGE SCOPE

Scope describes the boundaries of the project. It defines what the project will and will not deliver, what data is and is not needed, which organizations are affected and which are not, etc. Without proper scope definition, you have no chance to manage scope effectively.

The purpose of scope change management is to protect the viability of the current, approved Project Definition. When a project is defined, certain expectations are set as to what the project is going to produce, for what cost, and within what time frame. If the deliverables change during the project (and usually this means the customer wants additional items), then the estimates for cost, effort, and duration may no longer be valid. That is really the essence and purpose of scope change management—to ensure the initial agreements are met, and to ensure the project team and stakeholders agree to any changes to the expectations.

Different people can propose scope change requests. Before any changes to scope can be implemented, however, the impact on the project must be determined in terms of time, cost, and quality. The project manager can then present the proposed change, along with the overall impact of the change, to the project sponsor.

Scope change management is about managing change and ensuring the right people can make informed decisions. Sometimes the project manager thinks scope management means having to tell the customer "no." That makes the project manager nervous and uncomfortable. However, effective scope management is the art of getting the sponsor to say "no" (or even "yes").

STEP 6 MANAGE COMMUNICATION

Properly communicating on a project is critical to the success of managing customer and stakeholder expectations. If these people are not kept well informed of the project progress, there is a much greater chance of problems and difficulties due to differing levels of expectations. In fact, in many cases where conflicts arise, it is not because of the actual problem, but because the customer or manager was surprised.

Two typical forums for communicating status are through a status meeting and status reports. All projects should communicate status. This includes reporting from the project team to the project manager and reporting from the project manager to the customers and stakeholders. While small projects usually do not require much more than basic reporting, medium projects require a more formalized set of activities, and large projects require the most sophistication. This multifaceted approach is defined in a Communication Plan.

STEP 7 MANAGE RISK

Risk refers to future conditions or circumstances outside the control of the project team that will have an adverse impact on the project should they occur. In other words, an issue is a current problem that must be dealt with, whereas a risk is a potential future problem that has not yet occurred. Successful projects try to resolve potential problems before they occur. This is the art of risk management. Risk management is a proactive process invoked to eliminate potential problems before they occur, and therefore increase the likelihood of success on the project.

Since small projects usually do not have a long duration, there is not as much opportunity for problems. For medium and large projects, however, a complete assessment of project risk should be performed when the project is defined. A risk level should then be assigned to each risk identified, along with the likelihood the risk will occur. Risk plans are created for high-risk items with a potentially large impact on the project. Other combinations of high-to-medium risks, with high-to-medium likelihood, should also have risk plans prepared.

During the project, the project manager needs to monitor the risk plans to ensure they are being executed successfully. At the end of each phase or major milestone, the project manager also needs to perform an additional risk assessment based on current circumstances.

STEP 8 MANAGE DOCUMENTS

This step discusses the storing and sharing of electronic and paper documents. In general, the idea of document management is similar to computer source code management. These considerations are trivial for small projects, but for large ones, these processes need to be planned ahead of time, or confusion, uncertainty, and extra work will occur when the project is in progress.

The larger the project, the more rigor and structure needed to manage documents. If you do not think through a good document management plan ahead of time, you can end up with a big mess trying to save and find documents. Various factors need to be considered to successfully manage documents. These include where you will store the documents, how they will be organized, tools to use, access and security rules, keywords/indexing, naming standards, version management, completion status, retention/purging, backups, and standard template formats.

STEP 9 MANAGE QUALITY

Quality is ultimately defined by the customer, and represents how close the project and deliverables come to meeting the customer's requirements and expectations. Our goal is to meet the customer's requirements and expectations. This is a critical point. Sometimes there is a tendency to think "quality" means the best material, the best equipment, and absolutely zero defects. However, in most cases, the customer does not expect, and cannot afford, a perfect solution.

The purpose of the quality management step is to first understand the expectations of the customer in terms of quality, and then put a proactive plan and process in place to meet those expectations. A faulty process cannot produce a consistently high-quality product. There needs to be a repetitive cycle of measuring quality, updating processes, etc. To make the quality management process work, collecting metrics is vital.

One of the purposes of quality management is to find errors and defects as early in the project as possible. Therefore, a good quality management process will end up taking more effort hours and cost up front in the project. However, there will be a large payback as the project progresses. Small projects do not require much more than basic quality control, but for medium and large projects, a Quality Plan should be constructed to make sure the project is being completed to standards.

> ### STEP 10 MANAGE METRICS

Gathering metrics on a project is the most sophisticated project management process, and can be the hardest. Because metrics can be hard to define and collect, they are usually ignored. This is unfortunate because it is very difficult to improve the quality of your deliverables or your processes if you are not gathering metrics. Metrics are used to give some indication of what the beginning state of quality is, and whether quality is increasing or decreasing.

It is also worth noting that metrics management can be used effectively on medium/large projects because there is enough time to capture the data, analyze the results, and make appropriate changes. The most value is gained, however, if metrics are used to drive improvements on an organization-wide basis.

For the most part, small and medium projects should capture metrics across the entire organization. Depending on the organization, there may also be more information required for medium projects. Large projects should definitely capture metrics to provide information on the quality of the project and the processes used to create the deliverables. This process will result in the creation of a Project Scorecard. Steps to creating a Project Scorecard include identifying criteria for success, assigning potential metrics, looking for a balance, prioritizing the balanced list of metrics, setting targets, and adding workplan detail.

The Year Begins—on a Slippery Note

The snow was still falling, although lightly now and with fewer flakes, as I stared out the bedroom window on the morning of January 4. I could already smell the coffee brewing downstairs in the kitchen and longed to pour myself a cupful to warm my insides. But last night's snowstorm had made a mess of the driveway, and I knew the only way my family and I were getting out of the house today was to start digging now. The storm had deposited about six inches of heavy snow, and it took about an hour to carve a clear path from the garage to the street. Time to invest in a snowblower, I thought.

The morning shovel took much longer than anticipated, leaving me barely enough time to grab a shower and get dressed, let alone have breakfast with my now awake wife, Pam, and our 5-year-old son, Tim. Sensing my anxiety and realizing I was running late, Pam poured my coffee and cream into a cup-sized thermos and wrapped a couple pieces of toast in a paper towel to consume on the road. I grabbed both items, planted a kiss on Pam and Tim, and headed out the garage door to start my day.

I had barely driven a block when I felt the back end of my Volvo turn to the left, against my wishes, and begin skidding toward the curb. As I came to a stop, I could see in my rearview mirror the newly fallen flakes were secretly hiding patches of ice underneath. The day had just begun, and I had driven less than a half-mile from my house, but I knew one thing for certain—I was going to be late for my first day as project management advisor at Mega Manufacturing.

Mega Manufacturing was the nation's fifth largest manufacturer. I'd been working there for 10 years in the IT department, and was recently promoted to a new position as project management advisor. It was a good opportunity for me, and I was excited to use my knowledge of project management to help others in the company become more efficient and successful with their projects. When I took the job, I knew I would have an opportunity to work with many project managers—some well trained and highly experienced, and some brand new to the concept. Jerry Ackerman, I knew, was going to be part of the latter group. . . .

1

Jerry Doesn't Realize He Is Managing a Project

Jerry and I had scheduled a meeting prior to the company closing for New Year's Day, and I found him waiting outside my office when I arrived.

"Jerry, I am terribly sorry to be so la—"

"Tom! Good to see you," he interrupted. "Don't be silly about being late. I just got here 15 minutes ago myself."

"It took me longer than anticipated to get the snow shoveled this morning. I must be moving slower in my old age!"

"A shovel? We need to get you a snow blower!"

I smiled at his suggestion, recalling I had similar thoughts just a few hours earlier.

Jerry and his wife, Barbara, were trying to buy their first house, but the hunt for the perfect home had so far been long and difficult. He shared some of those struggles with me, and we talked at great length about the house my wife and I purchased a few years ago.

"The right house will come along, Jerry. Did you see any you liked this weekend?"

"Not really, Tom. We looked at a few open houses on Sunday, but the weather prevented us from looking at any more. We are trying to remain optimistic, but it's really starting to drive us crazy."

"Well, stick with it," I said, trying to sound reassuring.

Jerry was a relatively new employee who worked in the Information Infrastructure Department. He had big, blue eyes and a thick head of hair with shaggy sideburns. The sideburns and bushy hair gave him the slightly nerdish appearance that many people have come to expect of people who work with computers. If it was possible to tell such things based on a person's appearance, he also looked like the kind of person who liked to work with technology more than people. He had just been given the responsibility of upgrading the company's phone system, but wasn't sure he was ready for *the task. The work involved inspecting the phone lines, replacing the lines where needed, and upgrading the software. Jerry predicted the effort would take four months to complete and cost upwards of $350,000. There would be six people involved, although not all full time.*

After talking awhile longer about his house-hunting experiences, I asked Jerry if he wanted to talk a bit about his upcoming project.

"Sure," he said. "Actually, I am not sure there is anything you can help me with. Aren't you supposed to help project managers?"

I was initially taken aback, thinking I had perhaps missed something. "Well, yes. But it sounds like you have a pretty important project. Are you an experienced project manager?"

"Project? Project manager?" Jerry questioned, sounding unsure. "We don't do projects in this department. We just go ahead and get the work done."

The light bulb went off in my head, and I knew I was going to have my hands full. Not only is Jerry an inexperienced project manager, he doesn't even know he is the project manager!

"Jerry," I said, "let's talk."

LESSON 1

UNDERSTAND THE CHARACTERISTICS OF A PROJECT

All work typically falls into one of a handful of buckets:

- Support work is associated with keeping current production processes working and stable, such as fixing a crashed computer application.

- Operations work is associated with the ongoing execution of a company's business process, such as entering accounting transactions or ordering supplies.

- Overhead includes vacation and sick time.

- Management and leadership is associated with the time spent managing people and moving the organization forward to achieve its business goals.

Project work falls, for the most part, into the last category, which is the area of interest to me in my new job. Projects are not something only certain departments do—they are how work gets done. In fact, projects can exist in any functional area. This is a key difference between the work a person does and the organization where that person works. For instance, your support department may execute some projects as well as support-type work. Your operations area may execute projects as well as operations work. Your management team may even do projects, in addition to their management work. This highlights the difference between your functional group, for instance the support department, and the actual type of work you perform. Although there are differing definitions of projects, all projects have three major characteristics—a finite time frame, uniqueness, and deliverables.

First and foremost, a project must have a start and end date. Although one could quibble about exactly what the dates are, there must be a time before the work existed and there must be a time when the work no longer exists. Entering transactions into an accounting system, for instance, is not a project because the activity goes on indefinitely. Answering questions from the users about the accounting system software is not a project either, since those questions will be asked indefinitely as well. On the other hand, Jerry's work to upgrade the phone system was not happening before, and at some point it will be completed (even if it goes over its deadline, it will either be completed or cancelled). The phone system may be upgraded again, but if that happens, there will be a time gap between the upgrades, so the work is not continuous. The next upgrade will have a start and an end date as well.

All projects are also unique. They have unique characteristics, unique deliverables, unique people, and unique circumstances. As a contrast, if you worked for the help desk, over time you would begin to master your job, since there is a certain rhythm and pattern to the work. Once you get some experience, you find you can handle the repetitive nature of the work by following a certain set of processes and procedures. This is an example of ongoing operations. Working at the help desk today is similar to working there yesterday and it will be similar tomorrow and a year from tomorrow.

On the other hand, projects are unique. This characteristic makes them hard to estimate and hard to manage. Even if the project is similar to one you have done before, new events and circumstances will occur. Each project typically holds its own challenges and opportunities.

Lastly, all projects produce a specific set of deliverables. These deliverables could be anything from a computer application to an analysis document, from a recommendation to a new house. If the work does not result in the creation of one or more deliverables, then it is not a project. Even if your project were building a service, you would have deliverables such as a procedures manual, training classes, and perhaps marketing literature.

Most people also assign other characteristics to projects. These include a defined scope, a defined set of resources (people, money, equipment, supplies, etc.), common objectives (stated or unstated), and an assigned project manager and project team (although technically in a project team of one, these roles are filled by the same person).

It is important to note there are no upper or lower limits in terms of effort, cost, or duration. A project might take 10,000 hours to complete, or it might take 10 hours to complete. Very small projects are typically called *enhancements* or *discretionary requests*. Of course, how one manages these small and large projects is not the same. The 10-hour project probably does not have any formal project management techniques applied to it at all.

Projects can be found in all types of business—from marketing to manufacturing to movie studios. Yes, even in the Information Infrastructure Department where Jerry works! How many times have major initiatives failed because they were not organized and managed as a project? Many, many times. Jerry wants to just "get the work done." That type of thinking is fine for a 40-hour project where work can be planned and defined in your head. However, this initiative is too big, too complex, and too important for Jerry to manage in his head. He will have a better chance of success if he defines, structures, and manages the work as a project. When I meet with him next, the education process will continue.

2 | Ashley and the Disappearing Sponsor

The next day I had an opportunity to meet with Ashley Parker, the project manager on a large marketing information database project that was just beginning a major new phase. Ashley was married and had two children. She often volunteered at her kids' school and also helped out once a month at their neighborhood church. She was wearing dark pants with a plain red turtleneck and red-framed glasses when she came into my office at a little past 2 p.m. Good, solid business clothes—nothing fancy, but nothing odd either. On second look, the red glasses did give her a little bit of pizzazz. Her hair was shoulder length, and she stood about 5' 3", even with heels on. Solid image. I'd see how solid a project manager. I had known Ashley for about three years, although we had never really worked together before.

"Hello Ashley. How are you?" I asked as she entered my office.

"I am doing okay, I guess. Am I interrupting you?"

"Not at all," I replied. "Just filling out a form for new business cards."

Ashley smiled and sat down in the chair in front of my desk, while I pushed the order form aside for the moment. Ashley had a look of concern on her face, and I asked her to give me an update on her project. She informed me her team had just completed phase one of the project. The next phase needed to start right away, but she wasn't sure the business client was fully involved. The original business sponsor had recently been reassigned, and Ashley had not had a chance to meet the new manager in that role.

We discussed her situation for a few minutes.

"In today's rapidly changing business environment, it is not uncommon for companies to experience turnover of key project resources," I explained. "The marketing and sales department seems to have more people coming and going than most. That's one reason it makes sense to break large projects down into phases, each of which can be managed as an individual project. You are very smart to use this approach. Whenever you complete

13

one phase, you always have a chance for a checkpoint to make sure every-thing is ready to proceed to the next phase."

"Thanks," she responded.

"Did you complete a Project Definition document before the project started?" I asked.

"Yes, I did," she answered.

"How old is it?" I asked.

"It was written and approved four months ago," she replied.

"I assume your previous sponsor approved the project. Has the new sponsor seen the Project Definition?"

"I don't think so," Ashley responded. "He has so many things on his mind; I don't think our project is on his radar screen yet."

"You are entering a new phase," I confirmed with Ashley, who nodded. "Have you updated the Project Definition to reflect the new work?"

Ashley now shook her head. "We haven't been able to get the time we need from the sponsor and the client to validate the remaining work."

"Okay, the worst thing would be to continue the project without business involvement, and then have to redo much of the work later on—or even cancel the whole project for lack of sponsorship," I said. "Let's not keep things going based on their own momentum. Now is the time to revalidate business commitment and sponsorship, and make sure you are still on the right track. Then you can refocus the team for the next phase."

LESSON 2

MAKE SURE YOU ALWAYS HAVE AN IDENTIFIED AND COMMITTED SPONSOR AND CLIENT ORGANIZATION

The term *client* is used in multiple contexts. Sometimes, the term refers to a specific person and sometimes the term refers to the group of people receiving the project benefit. For instance, if you say, "The client asked us to include some new requirements," you may be referring to a specific person or you may be referring to the generic client organization.

Sponsors have ultimate authority over projects, and they are almost always within the client organization. In most companies, the simplest way to identify the sponsor is to ask who is providing funding for the work. The sponsor also resolves major issues and scope changes, approves major deliverables, and provides high-level direction. The sponsor acts as a champion for the project within his or her organization, and elsewhere as needed. If the project is large, and the sponsor is senior enough in the company, he or she may take on the role as executive sponsor, and delegate the day-to-day decision making to a lower-level project sponsor.

Typically, a project would not get funded or started without a sponsor. However, in some projects, the sponsor tends to sink into the background and does not remain actively engaged in the project. When that happens, the client organization can start to lose interest and focus as well. Good project managers should make sure this never happens. The sponsor should be kept as actively involved as possible. To accomplish this, project managers should meet with the sponsor regularly, keep him or her informed of project progress, and frequently ask for direction and advice.

Unfortunately, sponsors sometimes leave their companies in the middle of a project. This is the situation Ashley faces. She has a project in progress and is ready to move from one phase to the next. Many project managers would be tempted to just keep the project moving and continue working until someone tells them to stop. Ashley, however, recognizes that this is not right, because two very big problems can occur.

First, new sponsors have new ideas and new requirements. To a certain extent, that is the privilege of being the sponsor. Ashley wants to make sure she understands any differences between the desires of the old sponsor and the new one. Otherwise, she may end up having to perform more work later when the new sponsor finally has more time to pay closer attention.

Second, transitioning from one sponsor to another can lead to a lack of focus from the client organization. Ashley recognizes this as well since she told me her clients were not as engaged as they should be. This usually manifests itself in the form of unanswered phone calls, messages not returned, missed meetings, or missed deadlines. In Ashley's case the loss of focus from her client organization is probably directly related to the loss of her original sponsor.

It's not easy to stop a project, especially since the resources allocated to the project could become idle or could potentially be reassigned. However, Ashley cannot continue without an identified sponsor and client commitment. She should talk to her manager and the client manager about validating who the new sponsor will be, and getting him or her engaged soon. If the project is still important to the client, Ashley should be able to get a new sponsor involved, reenergize the client group, and continue the work. If she cannot get a new client sponsor, she and her manager need to put the project on hold. It would be a potentially painful step, but not as painful to the company as completing an irrelevant project. Once clients understand that a project will be put on hold, they will have to make a decision on its relevant importance. If it is important enough, it will receive the proper level of focus. If not, the project will probably not be continued.

3 Mike's Client Has Status Report Envy

STEP 6 MANAGE COMMUNICATION

Mega Manufacturing is headquartered in Dickens, Illinois, population 90,000. The laid-back town is located about 55 miles northeast of Chicago, and Mega Manufacturing is by far its leading industry. The second biggest source of jobs in the town is Northeast Illinois State University, a small liberal arts college with an annual student population of 8,000. Pam and I moved to Dickens 11 years ago when I was hired in Mega's IT department. Several months after we moved, the university hired Pam as ticket coordinator in its athletics department. She is currently sports information director for the university, a title she has held for the last three years.

Although fairly small, the town is genuinely charming and very beautiful, with many tree-lined streets and an open, inviting attitude. We tell our out-of-town friends our city is very "family friendly," with great schools, plenty of parks, and a low crime rate. And when we want to get away for the weekend, we just hop in the car and head for Chicago.

That's exactly what Mike Miller did over the weekend. He and his family spent Saturday and Sunday in Chicago, catching a Bulls game on Saturday night. Mike was a popular employee in our office, and had a great reputation as a patient, thoughtful man who would bend over backwards to help a friend or colleague. His office was full of family photos, with several pictures of his kids in their baseball uniforms, soccer uniforms, and his youngest daughter in a ballerina tutu. He had asked me to stop by on January 13 to discuss a project he was doing to install document management software in the Legal Department.

"How is life treating you Mike?" I asked as I entered his office.

"Oh, good and bad, Tom," he responded. "The kids and I just got back from a fun weekend in Chicago catching the Bulls crush the Cleveland Cavaliers. So that was good."

"And what's the bad?"

"Well, it's this darn project I am working on. That's why I asked you to stop by today. I could really use your advice, Coach."

I smiled. Mike had given me the nickname "Coach" at last year's annual New Year's Eve party when my transfer was announced. He liked to call people by nicknames, and I had to admit the practice carried a certain degree of charm and camaraderie. Mike always made you feel like a friend, even if you were meeting him for the first time.

"Give me some of the details Mike. What exactly is the problem?"

"My sponsor saw a report on the desk of the finance director showing the status on a big project underway in the finance area. He started to ask questions, and now it turns out I need to do a status report as well."

"Interesting," I said. "Sounds like you don't currently report status. Is that right?"

"No, we don't," Mike said. "Now my sponsor wants a status report like the one from finance. This report is four pages long and contains more detail than we track here. It's going to take us a long time to get the report done— time we could be spending working on the project."

I could see where this was leading. "Don't you consider communicating with your business clients part of your work on the project?" I asked.

"We were communicating fine without having to do a four-page status report. We always took time to let the client know what was going on whenever they asked. You know, it's all this paperwork that turns people against methodology."

"Project managers need to consider effective, proactive communication as part of their job," I replied. "But let's be clear; there is a difference between 'reporting status' and 'status reports.'"

LESSON 3

REPORT STATUS ON ALL PROJECTS (THERE ARE MANY ALTERNATIVES TO THE FORMAT AND DELIVERY)

Many years ago, a good project manager might have gotten away with being a poor communicator. The business clients typically didn't like it, but as long as project managers could deliver the goods, clients were inclined to let them do their own thing.

In today's world, however, projects need to be undertaken in partnership with clients, and the partnership absolutely requires solid communication. If you are managing a large project, you may have a multifaceted communication approach. On a smaller project, the communication needs are not as sophisticated. However, in large and small projects, the communication basics typically include status reporting.

Status reporting can take many shapes, depending on the size of project. The project manager may request that team members submit formal status reports on a weekly, biweekly, or monthly basis. These reports are usually summarized by the project manager and issued to his or her functional manager, as well as the sponsor and other stakeholders. These are typically written documents, although they could be e-mail messages or Web page updates. They could even be voicemail messages.

In addition to status reports, most projects also have some form of status meeting. Again, these could be at different levels. The project manager might have a weekly status meeting with members of the team, and a separate status meeting with sponsors, managers, and a steering committee. Typically one meeting will not suffice, since the level of detail and audience interest is vastly different between senior management and the project team.

The main function of status reporting is to communicate project accomplishments, as well as to highlight any major problems, scope changes, risks, etc. The purpose of status reporting is to manage expectations and to ensure that all participants and stakeholders have a common understanding of the project today, as well as what the future looks like. No one likes surprises. Proactive and ongoing communication is the key to making it all work.

It sounds like Mike does not see proactive communication as a core responsibility of the project manager. Mike is a reactive communicator. He says he provides a full status of the project whenever his sponsor asks for it, but what he doesn't realize is this lack of effective, proactive communication is exactly what is causing the sponsor to request additional information in the form of a formal status report.

My discussion with Mike centered around two main points:

- Proactive communication is absolutely part of the job of a project manager. The ability to proactively anticipate the communication needs of your stakeholders is one of the criteria separating casual project managers from mature and professional project managers.

- "Reporting status" is not the same as a "status report." Reporting status is something all project managers need to do. Status reports are just one delivery mechanism.

While the sponsor has requested a specific four-page status report he saw elsewhere, there are probably many alternatives. Mike should talk with the sponsor to determine what his information needs are, and then provide that information. Managers do not want to see the day-to-day minutia that is occurring on the project. They usually want you to stick to the major facts and tell them if they should be worried about anything. A common technique is to report the status of a project with an overall color code of green (okay), yellow (caution), or red (in trouble). Remember as well that the status report is a recap. If any major problems or events occur during the month, you should be communicating at the time of the occurrence.

Generally, your sponsor will be reasonable. If certain types of information are hard to report, chances are he or she will not require it. As mentioned earlier, there are many ways to report status. A formal status report document may not be needed at all.

Understanding the informational needs of your stakeholders is a part of communications planning. This should be done at the beginning of a project. Mike is playing catch-up now, but this experience should strengthen his understanding of this critical project management function so he can do better in the future.

4 | Lindsay Finds Activities Are Always 90 Percent Complete

STEP 3 MANAGE THE WORKPLAN

January 15 brought an unusual amount of excitement and happiness to the office, especially considering we had just been hit with our second big snow-storm of the year. I figured the joyful spirit was attributable to it being pay-day. I had heard a lot of people talking about overspending during the holidays and how they were in need of a financial shot in the arm. I, too, had spent more than I planned, and was excited to get my first paycheck as project management advisor. My promotion had brought a nice raise with it, but I wasn't sure what my new semimonthly compensation would be after taxes. I received my paycheck and, as expected, would not be able to retire early as a result of my raise. But I was not complaining. Every little bit helped.

Leaning back in my office chair, I picked up the framed picture I had on my desk of Tim as a newborn baby and stared in amazement at how little he was at birth and how quickly he was growing. He had bright green eyes like his mother and a big head like his dear old dad. I was still staring at his pic-ture when Lindsay Peterson arrived. Her quiet knock broke my trance, and I stood up quickly to greet her.

"Lindsay, come in, come in! Sorry I didn't see you right away."

"That's okay, Tom," she replied. "I find myself doing the same thing with my new girl."

Lindsay worked in the Application Support area and had recently returned from maternity leave after the birth of her daughter, Patricia, in November. Her husband, Al, was a carpenter by trade, and made quite a lot of money as an insurance contractor. I had not seen Lindsay in several months, but she looked much the same, with the exception of the noticeably black circles under her eyes. As a parent, I understood about sleepless nights with a newborn.

"So how is life with little Patricia?"

"You know, she is only two months old, but I already find it hard to remember life without her. She is such a wonderful little baby, and she brings so much joy to Al and me. We'll have to invite you and Pam over for dinner one night so you can see her."

I thanked her for the offer, and took a few minutes to peruse the pictures of Patricia she pulled from her purse. She was a cute baby with a round face and blue eyes. I was a little surprised to see she was bald, though, as Lindsay and Al both have full, thick heads of hair.

"So please, tell me about your project," I said, returning to my chair. Lindsay's Application Support team did not do projects often, but when they did, the projects tended to be complex. Her current project was a good example. She was managing a complex enhancement to a Sales Department application. They had the most knowledge of this package, since they supported it on an ongoing basis.

"I'm not sure what to do," she began. "I've got good people on the team, but we are falling behind schedule. Some team members have been unable to allocate the time required to get the work done on schedule. Most of them are trying to balance work on my project with their other support responsibilities. When the current release has problems, they need to shift time over for that."

"How are you managing the project plan and keeping track of end dates?" I inquired.

"Every Wednesday and Friday I ask the team to give me an update. I ask for the number of hours spent on each assigned activity, and what percent is complete. The problem is it seems that the work is always 90 percent complete. By the time it's 100 percent complete we have missed the deadline. When I talk to people about the project falling behind, they tell me they haven't been able to allocate the time the activity requires. If the activity takes 40 hours of effort, they don't consider it a problem unless they go over 40 hours. If it takes them a week longer to work all 40 hours, they still think they are doing okay."

I drilled a little deeper. "What is the purpose of asking people how many hours they worked on each activity?"

Lindsay was a little puzzled. "Having the team report hours tells me how much time they are spending on each project activity, and helps me to validate how close the original estimates were."

"Okay. I think you are getting that information," I agreed. "But it's not enough. You're falling behind. What information would be the most helpful for future project planning?"

She thought for a minute. "The deadline dates are really the most important. What I really want to know is when the work will be done."

LESSON 4

FOCUS ON DEADLINE DATES FIRST WHEN MANAGING A PROJECT

Have you ever managed a project where the work was always 90 percent complete? It seems everyone has. Usually after a period of frustration, you realize that asking people what percentage of work is complete is only of limited value.

Estimating effort hours is important in setting up the original schedule and determining completion dates. But once the workplan is created and activities are assigned, the focus should switch to getting the work done on time. This does not mean actual effort hours are unimportant. They are important—especially if you are charging a client on an hourly basis, or if the project team contains contract resources charged on an hourly basis.

However, in a typical internal project utilizing internal resources, it is easier and more effective to manage the project based on the assigned end dates. Then just one question needs to be asked and validated: When will the work be done?

Lindsay's project showcases a common scenario. An activity may have been estimated to take 40 effort hours and two weeks to complete. Of the two estimates, the more important aspect of success is whether the work was completed within the two weeks. To a certain extent, it really doesn't matter if the actual effort took 30 hours or 60—as long as it is completed within two weeks (assuming, of course, there are no charges for each excess hour of work). When Lindsay receives status updates from the team, she should validate whether each activity will be completed by its deadline. If team members think it will, then Lindsay is fine. If they don't think it will, then Lindsay can take corrective action if necessary.

Regardless of how diligent your team members are, some deadlines will still be missed. If the work is not complete, the project manager's question is still, When will the work be done? This line of questioning eliminates the problem of an activity being 90 percent complete, then 95 percent complete, then 99 percent complete—while the activity is one, two, and then three weeks late.

There are reasons for keeping track of percent complete and actual effort hours. However, for schedule management, focus on when the work will be done. Managing the effort hours and the dollars are two indicators of success, but managing by completion date is the best way to keep a project focused on its deadlines.

5 Susan's Small Enhancement Has Grown into a Project

STEP 1 DEFINE THE WORK

Susan Chang phoned me on January 19 and asked for a quick meeting the next day to discuss her manufacturing project. When I arrived at her office she was on the phone, although she motioned for me to come in. Susan had straight black hair she often wore pulled back with a clip or rubber band. She was born in Taiwan, but her parents were killed when she was a baby. An American soldier adopted her and brought her back to the States to live with him and his wife in Dickens. She was now in her early 30s. My knowledge of her came mostly from other people, although I did chat with her briefly at the New Year's Eve party, where she told me some of her background. Taking my seat, I could hear her saying "Mommy needs to go now sweetie," and I knew she must have been talking to one of her kids. After she hung up, she explained her youngest was feeling ill and had stayed home sick from school.

"She wanted to call and tell me her grandma was going to make her grilled cheese and chicken soup for lunch. She just loves grilled cheese."

"That's funny," I said. "How long has she been sick?"

"Only a few days," she replied. "It's just a cold, but you know how quickly those germs can spread. We figured it would be in everyone's best interest to keep her home for a few days."

The one thing I did know about Susan was she was a germ freak. She kept little moist towelettes in her desk drawer to wipe off the phone and doorknobs periodically, and she also washed her hands more than anyone else I know.

"Probably best," I offered. "So tell me, Susan, what's going on with your project?"

"Well, our client is very upset with us right now," she began. "The client's request started off simply enough. First, we were asked to create a new report to show the manufacturing run rate over the previous three months.

Then, as we were finishing this off, he decided he wanted us to estimate the run rates over the next three months as well."

"Did you note this as a scope change?" I asked.

"No," Susan replied quickly. "We do not do projects in our group—just small enhancements. The original request should have only taken us 20 hours to complete. That's the typical size of the enhancements we perform."

I thought for a second about her comment "We do not do projects in our group" and was instantly reminded of my prior meeting with Jerry a few weeks back.

"That's fine for the initial request," I replied. "But how about the changes the client is asking for now?"

Susan hesitated for a few seconds. "That was a more complex piece of work requiring a few extra weeks. We did not have all of the data we needed, so we had to make some changes to capture the right information. We also had some trouble understanding how the new report should be calculated."

I was starting to get the picture. "Okay, how much time has been spent on this?"

"It is hard to say," she answered. "But we've had one to two people assigned to this for the last six weeks."

Six weeks! No wonder the client is unhappy, I thought.

LESSON 5

APPLY SOME LEVEL OF PROJECT MANAGEMENT DISCIPLINE—EVEN ON SMALL PROJECTS

This situation occurs all the time. You start off with a small request that seems like a piece of cake. Then, before you know it, you have spent weeks and hundreds of hours on it. How did you end up in such straits? You might have just misunderstood and underestimated the original request. But what's more likely is that the original, simple request has become more complicated thanks to additional changes, additions, and revisions from the client.

Earlier, when I defined a project, I said enhancements are considered projects because they have a beginning and an end, they result in a deliverable, and they have resources applied. An enhancement that takes 1,000 hours to complete is easy to categorize as a project. However, Susan's small enhancement fits the definition of a project as well.

If this was a formal project, Susan would have developed a Project Definition document that included a description of scope. Of course, Susan cannot be expected to manage a 20-hour request as a formal project. These types of projects can be planned and managed in her head. However, Susan did not recognize the fact that her request had evolved from a 20-hour project into one that will take hundreds of hours to complete. At this point, the work has already consumed several weeks and a couple hundred hours—and it is not over yet! Looking back, the work definitely should have been run as a small project.

How should you manage work that starts off very small, but ends up being much larger? The answer is to manage small requests informally, but use the appropriate project management techniques when necessary. In Susan's case, when she received the major scope change, she should have performed some basic scope change management. If Susan did not understand the impact, she should have asked for time to further investigate. She could have then done a more complete analysis of the new work and created a new estimate of the effort hours and duration required to complete the changes. She would then have had more solid information to take back to the client to validate that he understood the impact of the changes in terms of time and effort.

If she had talked to the client and explained to him the consequences, he could have made a decision as to whether the incremental value of the request was worth the extra time and effort. This would have been a good use of informal scope change management.

When the work became larger, Susan should have also started communicating better, creating weekly status updates to better manage the client's expectations. In many cases, it is not the time delays the client is upset about; it is the lack of communication explaining the status and the challenges. Again, if the client was better informed as to the consequences of his request, he may have realized earlier that the request was not worth this level of effort.

It does not usually make sense to stop a small piece of work and go through a formal project planning stage when the work starts to grow. However, that assumes the change only requires an incremental increase in effort and time. If the manager does not know what the impact to the project will be, he or she should be prepared to invoke scope change management. If the work ends up being more substantial than originally thought, other project management practices may come into play, including better defining the work, building a simple workplan, and formally managing scope, issues, and communication.

6 | Jerry Starts to See the Light

I had been looking forward to my second meeting with Jerry for several days. His office was in a separate wing of our building, and I rarely saw him during the day. In fact, I had only seen him in person once since our initial meeting and that was in the first-floor cafeteria. We were both grabbing a quick sandwich before afternoon meetings.

Jerry was still finding his way at Mega Manufacturing, and was still a novice when it came to project management. We had been e-mailing each other a couple times a week for the last three weeks, and I was really beginning to feel like part of his team. Although I was not doing any of the work related to his upgrade of the phone mail system, I did feel like I was part of the planning process, advising Jerry on how best to get the job done. I had a personal stake in seeing Jerry and his project succeed, because I felt advising him was exactly why I was given the position as project management adviser.

Jerry and I had agreed to meet for lunch, and I was reading the morning paper when I saw him come into the lunchroom. I usually eat lunch at my desk unless I am meeting with someone, so relaxing and reading the paper seemed like a luxury.

"Hey Jerry. Glad to see you again," I said as I shook his hand.

"Good to see you again, too, Tom. Thanks for all the help you've been providing. I really appreciate it."

"Not a problem. I am glad to be of help. How are you doing?"

"Well, I am beginning to feel a bit overwhelmed, to be honest with you. This is partly because of this project and partly because of our house frustrations."

"You guys still haven't found a house?"

"No. In fact, we have lost a little bit of our enthusiasm about it. My wife is busy at her job, too, so we have not been able to devote a lot of time and

energy to it lately. We read the Sunday newspaper, and our realtor will call every now and again with something she thinks we should look at, but nothing has really panned out."

"What sort of things are you looking for?"

"Well, Barbara would like to have an older home, something with some charm and character. But we both like some of the modern conveniences like central air and heat and newer kitchens. We would also like a big master bedroom, and we both seem to like more open and spacious floor plans. It's amazing how many homes in Dickens don't have central air conditioning. I guess it's hard to think about that now since it is so cold. But come the summer, it gets so hot and humid here."

"Sounds like you both know what you want. I am sure if you keep looking, you will find something."

Jerry and I began eating our lunches and talked a bit more about houses. In time, the conversation turned back to work, and we began discussing his phone mail project. I could tell he was struggling with the ideas behind project management, and still wanted to focus his attention on "just getting the work done." Unfortunately, I had been hearing some complaints around the office about the initial progress of the team's work, and I thought it was important to address this right away.

"So, tell me, how are things progressing with your project?" I asked, putting down my turkey sandwich.

"Everything is going well. We have made some good progress."

"I'm sure you have," I replied. "But I heard there was some trouble when you tried to rewire the second floor. My understanding is that many people were disrupted because they lost phone access for two days."

"Yes, but it wasn't totally our fault," he protested quickly. "We didn't realize we had to do both sides of the floor. We thought that only half the phone lines needed to be rewired."

"You and I have been discussing the need for planning more before your team jumps in to begin working. Do you think more planning would have helped in this case?"

Jerry realized where my question was heading. His initial paradigm about "just doing the work" was now open to a better alternative.

LESSON 6

DEFINE AND PLAN THE WORK FIRST TO ENSURE BETTER PROJECT EXECUTION

It is not uncommon to have a debriefing session at the completion of a project (for projects with cost, quality, or delivery date problems, these meetings are sometimes called *postmortems*). When the team discusses the reason for problems, a common theme seems to dominate—a general lack of definition and planning. A common lament is, "If we had spent more time understanding the work, expectations, deliverables, scope, and risks, the results could have been different."

All projects should start with an up-front definition and planning process. If it's a small project, the process does not have to be elaborate. On the other hand, if it's a very large project, the planning process itself could take many months and thousands of hours. The time spent adequately planning the work will be more than made up for by a smoother running and more focused project over the long term.

The up-front work involves two separate objectives. The first is to define the work. This is the process of defining objectives, scope, risk, assumptions, etc. This information needs to be documented by the project manager and approved by the project sponsor to ensure there is a common understanding.

The second activity is to plan the work by building a project workplan. This lists the activities, the estimated length, the estimated effort, the resources applied, the dependencies between the activities, etc. The workplan is your best guess as to how the work will be completed.

It's a shame, but sometimes you need to stumble before you understand the importance of looking at where you are walking. In the same respect, even though I had talked to Jerry about defining and planning, he never really bought into the value until now. Before today, he was polite and tried to follow some of what I was suggesting, but I could tell his heart was not in it.

When we discussed the problem he encountered rewiring the second floor, Jerry suddenly realized that more planning and a better understanding of what was required for this portion of the project might have avoided the mistake. Now I sense Jerry will try harder to plan the remainder of the project, instead of just giving it lip service.

7 Poor Reyna—Trapped in Workplan Minutia

After my first month on the job, I felt like things were going very well. I had met with many people at Mega Manufacturing, and I felt my work was helping people to save valuable time, while also making the company money in increased productivity. I was also further strengthening an old friendship with Wayne Moretti, a vice president and also my new boss. Wayne and I went back a long way. He hired me as an associate IT specialist right out of college, when we both lived and worked in New York, and took an interest in my professional growth and development. Later, after I had moved to Atlanta and Wayne had moved to Dickens, he convinced me to relocate back to the Midwest and join him at Mega Manufacturing. After a long career, Wayne announced last December that he would be retiring this year at the age of 60.

It was Wayne who first talked to the CIO about staffing a position to help people manage projects. The IT department at Mega Manufacturing realized it needed to manage projects in a better way. The medium-term direction was to build a Project Management Office and utilize a common set of project management processes throughout the organization. However, budget cutbacks and competing priorities have pushed this off for one year. This year Wayne was able to gain approval for a project management advisor—me. After discussing the position with Wayne for a couple weeks, I decided to accept it. Wayne's backing gave me instant credibility in the office, and I found myself very busy quickly.

Before I stepped into this role, Wayne spent time mentoring project managers in his department, but he felt he was only moderately successful. He did not feel he had the focused time or the right level of project management competency himself to be a strong mentor. One of the people Wayne worked with was Reyna Andersen. Reyna was a few months into a large project to implement the first phase of a basic customer relationship management

(CRM) package at our company. Wayne wanted me to meet with her to begin offering her counsel when needed.

"Why don't you tell me about your current situation?" I asked Reyna when we met in her office Monday morning. "Wayne told me you ran into a little glitch."

"Well, when I built the workplan, I added a 15 percent allocation for project management work," Reyna began. "But I find myself spending more time than that. The workplan administration is really adding up. I am assigning work, following up to make sure it is completed, and updating the workplan. But it seems that's all I ever do."

I asked Reyna if I could have a look at the workplan. She handed me a stack of paper almost too painful to hold. "Wow!" I exclaimed, as I thumbed through the workplan. "You have more than 1,200 activities listed over the next four months."

"Well, it is comprehensive," Reyna replied proudly. "I want to make sure I understand the work to be done, and that my team does as well."

"You do need to understand the work to be done," I agreed. "Your team members need to understand as well. But you are probably giving them more direction than they need. For instance, I see an activity for setting up a biweekly meeting. Why do you have five subtasks for this activity?"

Reyna gave me the detailed response. "Well, you have to determine the participants, perform a calendar search, get a conference room, schedule the free time, and notify everyone."

"You're right, those all are steps to setting up a meeting," I concluded. "But remember what you said about understanding the work to be done? Don't you think if you just had one activity for setting up the meeting, you and your team would still know what to do?"

LESSON 7

DON'T "MICROBUILD" OR MICROMANAGE THE WORKPLAN

There is no hard-and-fast rule to describe what level of detail you should use to define activities in your workplans. Generally, there are two rules of thumb when it comes to defining the level of detail in the workplan.

First, as Reyna suggested, the workplan must be at a level where both the project manager (Reyna) and the project team can understand the work. That is why the workplan may be at different levels of granularity for different activities. If a piece of work is well understood, it can be placed on the workplan at a higher level. However, if it is not clear what the nature of the assignment is, then the activity should be broken down into its more basic components (in some companies, these lowest-level statements are called *tasks*). The project manager may even need to have a meeting with other team members to determine exactly what needs to be done for some larger activities.

The second rule of thumb is that the workplan must include time to react if an activity is in trouble. In general, an activity should never be longer than 80 hours (two weeks). This means if you assign an activity to be completed in 80 hours, you should know in two weeks whether the activity is completed (perhaps longer than two weeks if the resource is not working on it full time). If it is not completed, then you have time to address any problems and take corrective action.

This 80-hour limit is a good rule of thumb if you are working on a typical six-month project. However, what if your project is two months long? In that case, the 80-hour rule may not be appropriate because you may not have enough time for corrective action once you determine an activity is late. If you assign an 80-hour activity with a deadline of three weeks, your project may be almost half over before you fully realize there is a problem. Since the project is so short, a better high end for an activity might be 40 hours. Likewise, if you have a very short project of one month, perhaps no activity should be greater than 20 hours. In all of these cases, if you have an activity that requires more effort or duration than your threshold, you need to break the larger activity into one or more smaller activities.

Reyna likes to control things, but she is not following the first rule mentioned previously. She is not leaving the workplan at a level where the project manager and team members understand the activities. Reyna has fallen into the trap of building the workplan at too discrete a level. This has caused it to become inflated, cumbersome, and very hard to manage. Adding ten activities to the workplan where five will suffice (or perhaps one) adds extra work from a planning perspective and from a management perspective. Updating the workplan takes much longer, and making sure that the remainder of it ties together is much more difficult. The worst part is the extra activity produces very little incremental value, and is, in fact, detrimental. Reyna does not need that level of detail to manage the work and her team does not need that level of detail to understand what is needed.

Reyna has allocated 15 percent of the project budget toward project management activities. This should be plenty. She needs to free up more of her time by simplifying the workplan dramatically. When she does, she will still be able to control the project, but she will free herself up from the reactive drudgery caused by overadministering the workplan.

If you feel you are spending too much time managing the workplan and assigning work, you may be right. Make sure you are managing work at a level where you and your team members can understand the work assignments, while at the same time maintaining proactive control so that you can respond appropriately if problems arise.

8 Jerry Learns Firsthand the Need to Manage Documents

On February 7, I asked Jerry to stop by my office to discuss the current status of his project to upgrade the phone mail system. I was also anxious to share with him the news regarding the Morettis' house going on the market. He was wearing a light brown sweater when he walked into my office, and it looked like he had his hair cut recently. It was still shaggy, but not as shaggy as usual.

"Have a seat Jerry. I have really been looking forward to meeting with you today."

"Why is that Tom?" he asked with a puzzled look on his face.

"Tell me, have you guys had any luck finding a house?"

Jerry talked for five minutes on the continuing struggle he and his wife were having. They were only looking at houses every other weekend now, and were fast growing weary of the hunt. I was trying hard to listen to his concerns, but finally I could not hold back any longer.

"Jerry, I might have found the perfect house for you guys!"

He could tell I was excited and asked me to tell him the story. I gave him all the information I could think of on Wayne's house, and I could see Jerry's expression growing brighter and brighter the more I talked. I agreed to meet him and his wife for lunch on Sunday, and bring them by the Morettis' house so they could have a quick tour. He was so excited that he almost left to call his wife before we could discuss his phone mail project. I convinced him to stay a few minutes longer and to brief me on the status of his project.

"So, how have things been going on your project? Are you finding it valuable to plan before you work?" I asked.

"Yes, after the problems we had last month, we actually took the time to better define and plan the work as you suggested. I figured it was better late than never. Unfortunately, I made an embarrassing mistake that you may have heard about," Jerry replied sheepishly. "I was excited about sending my

Project Definition out for approval, but when I e-mailed it to the sponsor and my manager I sent them an old version of the document. The sponsor actually approved the document, but my manager saw that there were sections missing and that the budget and deadline were way out of line. So I had to send it back out a second time."

"Normally that wouldn't be so bad," I said. "But I heard the sponsor was quite embarrassed. I guess she did not read it very closely, and it showed when she signed the bad one."

"You're right," Jerry agreed. "She looked bad signing a document she hadn't read. She was not too happy with me."

"I guess the good thing is by the time you finish this project, you will have experienced many of the problems associated with project management. You're going to be an expert!" I said, trying to be funny. "Now, as far as this little glitch is concerned, how are you storing your documents?"

"I'm storing all of the internal project documents in a shared folder on the server. I have a central folder for holding everything related to the project."

"How did the documents get screwed up?" I asked.

"A stupid mistake," he replied, shaking his head disappointedly. "I e-mailed an early draft of the Project Definition to a team member for feedback. She then stored the document in the same shared folder with a slightly different filename. When I sent the final document out, I forgot the name of the original document and sent out the old draft version instead."

"This is not an unusual problem," I replied. "The larger the project, and the more people assigned to a project team, the more discipline and rigor is needed in the management of project documentation and knowledge."

LESSON 8

MANAGE DOCUMENTS PROPERLY TO AVOID CONFUSION AND MIX-UPS

One of the more sophisticated aspects of managing a project is to manage the flow of documentation. Small project teams normally do not need to put a lot of effort into document management. However, sharing information becomes increasingly complicated as a project team gets larger. Document management tools can help to enforce many of the rules for sharing documents, but most companies still rely on manual processes.

Jerry is probably managing his project documentation in the same way as the majority of project managers (the Legal Department at Mega has a project to implement document management software, but no one else in the company does as far as I know). The documents for a project start out in a shared folder accessible to all team members. If a project manager gets tired of looking for stuff, he or she might even define a set of subfolders for various categories of documents. This is actually the start of document management, but it is only the beginning.

The purpose of document management is to avoid having documents overwhelm you. On many projects, the project manager does not see the need to manage this aspect of the project until he or she can't find the important documents needed, or until an important document gets lost. The best practice is for project managers to consider the amount of documentation their project will generate before the project starts. If you plan to have status reports, workplans, scope change requests, etc., give some thought to document management before the start.

Document management can involve very simple and practical things. For instance, if your document names start with the date in year-month-day format, you can easily sort them in chronological order. If each team member has a subfolder for his or her work in progress, then draft clutter can be kept out of the main libraries. Another example is to add "draft" to the document name of a draft copy, and "final" to the end of a final version. These procedures can all be defined ahead of time.

For Jerry's project, having a shared folder to hold information is a good start. He also needs to have a well-thought-out directory structure, including a work area for each team member. Then he needs some simple rules about what types of documents are stored in each folder, as well as rules that define who is responsible for updating each folder. Like many other processes, planning the document management process up front will save much more time and confusion as the project progresses. In addition, once good document management processes are set up, the project manager can utilize them quickly on subsequent projects as well. The best approach is for your company to establish some guidelines and templates that can be easily and consistently used by default by all project managers in the organization.

9 Danielle Takes Scope Definition to Heart

I purposely scheduled all my meetings for the beginning of the day on February 14. I always bought Pam a dozen roses for Valentine's Day, and I liked to leave work early to stop by the florist. I wanted to leave especially early today because I was also planning a romantic dinner for the evening. My last appointment was with Danielle Bartlett, a young, single woman who had been with the company for about four months. She was wearing a black sweater and black pants, and looked a little glum when she entered my office.

"Why all black?" I asked as she sat down.

"I hate Valentine's Day," she said, trying to smile. "Actually, let me rephrase. I hate being single on Valentine's Day!"

Danielle seemed like a nice enough woman and I wanted to offer her some reassurance, but I didn't know her very well, and I didn't think anything I said would make her feel better, so instead we talked about work. She was beginning the early stages of a construction cost-estimating system for the Facilities Department, and she had e-mailed me a draft of her Project Definition document. I thought a few areas needed more work, including more definition and clarity around the project scope.

"Danielle, I've heard different people talk about the benefits of this cost-estimating package and it seems like everyone has a different idea about what the final solution will look like. But, when I read your scope statement, it left me with more questions than answers."

"I've defined the scope as best I know it," she replied. "I've stated that we will be implementing a tool to help estimate costs on major construction projects. It seems pretty clear to me."

"Well, I wonder if it is clear to the people reading the Project Definition," I said. "First of all, are you clear on whether the tool will be available worldwide or just in the U.S. division?"

"That's an easy one," she answered. "Other countries have different construction rules and regulations. Initially, we will use the tool for U.S. construction projects. It may be customized for other countries later."

"Okay," I said. "Your business client is the Facilities Department. But I've also heard that the tool might be of use in the Capital Accounting Group, so they can allocate costs more effectively to the appropriate capital accounts."

Again, Danielle had the answer. "My sponsor said I did not have to worry about the accounting implications. If they want to leverage the package, they will need to wait until the initial implementation is completed."

I had one more question to drive home the point. "I also heard people like the idea of being able to use the tool on their laptop. Then they can enter information when they are at the construction site and update it in real time."

Danielle was getting the picture. "Actually, the standalone capability will be available in a subsequent upgrade product. By the way, I get your point. Given the different expectations people have for this project, I guess the original scope statement was pretty vague."

LESSON 9

DEFINE THE MANY ASPECTS OF WHAT IS IN SCOPE AND OUT OF SCOPE

Scope can be thought of as a box defining the boundaries of a project. The work your project is responsible for is inside the box. The work you are not responsible for is outside the box. If you showed a box to people and asked them to describe it, some people would just say it was square. Those who were more geometrically inclined might say it was a cube. However, you will also find some observant people who would describe the size of the box, the color, the thickness, and what the box is made of.

Managing scope is one of the biggest challenges project managers face. It is much harder, in fact maybe impossible, if you have not done a good job defining scope to begin with. When you define the scope of your project, you are defining the characteristics of this "box" and what is in it. Further clarification of scope can be accomplished by clearly stating what is out of the box as well.

A good project manager would be wise to remember the box analogy the next time he or she needs to define the scope of a project. The scope definition should make it clear to the reader exactly what the project is trying to achieve. It should also clearly articulate what is out of scope, especially if there are areas of potential confusion. The project manager should think about the aspects of scope where people may have questions, and then identify which aspects are in scope and out of scope. Since Danielle is defining an IT project, she might also define scope in the following terms:

- What specific deliverables are in scope and out of scope?
- What organizations are in scope and out of scope?
- What major capabilities will the solution enable, and what are some obvious ones the project will not address?
- What data or databases are in scope and out of scope?
- What will this specific project deliver, and what will be delivered in subsequent related projects?
- Which business processes will be addressed and which ones will not?

Danielle's scope statement is very typical of how some project managers define project scope. It is brief and to the point, but it also leaves questions in the minds of the readers. Remember, the purpose of defining scope is to clearly articulate what you are taking responsibility for delivering on the project. You don't want to define your project, gain sponsor approval, and then still have questions arise later about exactly what is included in your project.

Based on the little I know of Danielle's project, I have already identified three areas where she should further clarify what is in scope and out of scope. There may be more as well. The good news is she knows the information. However, she is not sharing the information and being clear to the reader. She should be much clearer about what locations and organizations will be included in the initial deployment. Because there is some confusion in other related organizations, she should state specifically that the accounting group and other groups are out of scope. She should also be clear about the major features and capabilities that will and will not be included. The scope statement is not the place to put requirements, but the question of whether the solution can be used with a laptop sounds like it is an area of potential confusion. By being clear in the up-front scope definition, Danielle can better manage expectations and better manage the scope change process during the project.

10 | Patrick Discovers the Three "Best Friends" of Project Managers

STEP 1 DEFINE THE WORK

I pulled our car slowly into the driveway on Baker Street and squinted at the front door in an attempt to determine if this was, indeed, Wayne's house. Pam and I had been here several times before, but the house next to Wayne's looked similar from the outside and I always got them confused. The Morettis had invited us over for dinner, along with another couple and, as usual, we were early. I grabbed the bottle of wine we had purchased from the back seat and headed toward the front door.

Wayne greeted us and led us into the kitchen where his wife, Elsie, was busy cooking. The Morettis' house was warm and cozy, a combination of "old world" charm and modern-day conveniences. Wayne liked to have the newest gadgets and gizmos, and his home certainly reflected it. He took the most pride in showing off his basement, complete with big screen TV, pinball machine, pool table, bar, leather recliners, and fireplace. He collected beer steins, and they were prominently displayed on several walls and shelves.

Wayne had just opened our bottle of wine when the doorbell rang. Elsie greeted the new guests and brought them into the kitchen where Wayne introduced them as the Henleys—Patrick and Carolyn. Patrick was a manager in the finance division at his company, and Carolyn was a kindergarten teacher. Wayne asked all of us to sit around the dining room table and talk, while Elsie brought out several appetizers. She also poured glasses of wine for the Henleys.

Patrick and I sat next to each other at the table, and after a bit of small talk began discussing his job. It turned out he was responsible for managing a project to implement new finance procedures for the accounting department at his company. The work had been going on for three months. Obviously, his work struck a chord with me and I was excited to learn more.

"The project has taken longer than I originally estimated," Patrick admitted. "We seem to be trying to hit a moving target. First, we were just going to implement some additional auditing processes. Then we were asked to update the company chart of accounts. Now they want us to stan-dardize the entire auditing process. The original project was estimated for completion in two months. My manager keeps asking me when the work will be done, but how can I know when they keep adding more? She is anx-ious for us to finish so she can start us on a new project of interest to her."

"Interesting," I replied. "Given the three months you have invested already, and the scope changes you have picked up, how much of the project is left to complete?"

"Well, that depends on the accounting users," he explained. "If they accept our team's recommendations for the auditing process, the work might be completed in another two months or so. However, based on what we have done so far, the target always seems to be changing. Just as we think we are making progress, we find out something else needs to change. Just last week, for instance, we found out that the auditors now want us to com-pare our auditing practices against others in our industry."

"Do you have anything written down describing what you are doing or what your client is asking for?"

I knew the answer before I asked it. "No," he said.

Again I thought back to Jerry and Susan. Looks like they "don't do proj-ects" in Patrick's area either, *I thought.*

LESSON 10

USE THE "BIG THREE" DOCUMENTS—PROJECT DEFINITION, PROJECT WORKPLAN, AND REQUIREMENTS—AS THE FOUNDATION FOR YOUR PROJECT

Processes associated with managing a project have little value if you don't know what you are delivering and how you are going to do it. That is why the up-front definition and planning processes are so valuable. You can be the greatest workload manager in the world, but you are going to fail if you don't have agreement on what you are delivering and what it takes to get the work done. There are three major documents that build this founda-tion for a project—the Project Definition, the project workplan, and the business requirements.

The Project Definition (also called a project charter) defines the project deliverables, scope, assumptions, risks, costs, timelines, approach, etc. It is absolutely vital to have this document in place before you start the project work. Remember, this does not have to be a 30-page document. Scalability is still the rule. Small projects may be defined in a couple pages. Enhancement requests might need just one page. However, it is important to gain agreement with your business client on the work to be accomplished. If you cannot easily gain consensus on what the project is delivering, then it is even more vital that the work waits until agreement is reached. The Project Definition also communicates the project essentials to other stakeholders for their agreement and feedback as well.

The project workplan describes how you will execute the project, including building and deploying the deliverables. You may be able to plan out the activities for a small project in your head. However, as projects get larger, the workplan needs to be documented in a tool of some kind (or even a piece of paper). The workplan allows you to estimate the overall schedule and timeline, and helps you see the critical path of work driving the deadline.

Once the workplan is built, it must be kept up to date so that you can tell whether you are getting behind. An updated workplan also tells you how much work is remaining to complete the project.

The business requirements describe in more detail the characteristics, features, and functions of the deliverables. The Project Definition names the main deliverables of the project so that you can define the overall scope. However, the details and characteristics of the deliverables are not in the Project Definition. Normally, this level of detail is not known when the Project Definition is created. The business requirements describe the details of the deliverables so that you can design and build them correctly. Gaining approval on this document also ensures that a common set of expectations with the business client exists. If you do not have defined and approved requirements, you will find it difficult to manage scope effectively.

Looking at Patrick's project, it is clear he has not yet established the project foundation. He has no definition, workplan, or requirements. Consequently, he is not able to control scope (which would be in the Project Definition), he does not know how much work is remaining (from the workplan), and he is not sure how to build the deliverables (from the business requirements). It is not possible to know how much work is left, or whether he is on the right track.

Given the track record of the project so far, the best advice is for Patrick to pause the project and do a quick Project Definition, workplan, and requirements document. This will validate whether Patrick and his client are in agreement on the work remaining, what that work looks like, and how much time and effort it will take to accomplish the work. If he is on the right track, he should be able to resume his work and take the project to completion. If he is not on the right track, then the sponsor can decide whether the work should proceed given the effort required to get it back on track. Right now, no one can make an informed decision, since there is no agreed upon information on which to base a decision.

11 Jerry's Project Takes a Turn for the Worse—Maybe

STEP 5 MANAGE SCOPE

Jerry and I met on February 22 in my office to discuss his phone mail project, as well as his housing situation with the Morettis. Jerry and Barbara had visited Wayne and Elsie several times since our initial meeting and house tour, and Jerry and Wayne had begun talking about the price. Jerry seemed energized by his housing success, and he thanked me repeatedly for connecting him with Wayne. We talked at great length about his plans for moving in over the summer, and he made a special point of telling me that Wayne had agreed to leave his pool table and pinball machine as "housewarming" gifts. I thought he would talk forever about the house, but eventually I focused his attention on work-related matters. After four weeks of work, the phone mail system was going through some initial pilot testing.

"As we have been checking the phones and the wiring, we have also been working on the new voicemail software. We have the software in pilot test now and the test is going smoothly," Jerry began. "But yesterday, we received a request to change the call forwarding feature. The pilot team says it is more confusing to use than the old version, and they want the old functionality back."

"If I remember your Project Definition, you stated you were going to implement the new upgrade as is, with no custom modifications," I replied. "If your clients are requesting changes to the software, it sounds like a scope change request to me."

"You're right," Jerry agreed, "but it's not only a scope change; it's also a distraction. The vendor's first estimate is that the change will take two extra weeks, and cost us around $10,000. Then we will have to retest to make sure nothing else was broken. In addition, this slightly customized version of the software may cause us more problems down the road. I really wish we didn't have to do it."

I was sympathetic to Jerry's concerns, but I had an idea where this would all end up. "I don't think your situation is as bad as you think," I suggested. "You have enough information about the impact on the project to talk to your sponsor. First, make sure she is willing to proceed with the change."

"Good idea," Jerry said hopefully. "I'll try to have a short meeting with her this afternoon."

Later that day Jerry called me. "Well, I just had a great meeting with the sponsor," he said in an upbeat tone.

"And what did she say about making the change the pilot team recommended?" I asked.

"She emphatically told me 'Forget about it!'" Jerry replied, sounding more relaxed. "She said the new upgrade might be different, and it may not be perfect, but it is good enough!"

Just as I thought, I said to myself.

LESSON 11

USE SCOPE CHANGE MANAGEMENT TO ALLOW THE SPONSOR TO MAKE THE FINAL DECISION (MANY TIMES THE SPONSOR WILL SAY "NO")

There are two major reasons why projects have problems. The first is a basic lack of up-front definition and planning. The second is poor scope change management processes. Remember that scope refers to the box that defines the work of your project. The boundaries of the box separate the areas your project will be responsible for (in scope) versus those areas your project will not be responsible for (out of scope). Defining scope allows you to ensure you have an agreement with your sponsor on the "box" your project is responsible for. Defining scope also provides the baseline against which you can perform scope change management throughout the project.

Scope change management is necessary to protect the initial agreement you have with the sponsor. In the Project Definition, you agree to deliver a certain set of products for a certain level of effort, cost, and duration. If the basic nature of the products change, it is reasonable to expect the associated cost, effort, and duration to complete the work may change as well.

One of the conflicts project managers face is that they don't want to say "no" to someone who asks for a scope change. The requestor could be a client manager, stakeholder, or end user. If the requestor asks for changes, the project manager usually feels an instinct to say, "Yes, we can do it." Somehow, saying "no" to the request is seen as not being client focused, or not satisfying the client's needs.

The beauty of scope change management, however, is that the project manager does not have to be the "no" guy. In fact, the project manager does not need to decide one way or another. That is not the job of a project manager. The project manager's job is to identify the request and take it through the scope change management process. This includes evaluating the impact of the change on the project, looking at alternatives, and taking the information to the project sponsor for resolution.

Sponsors should make decisions on scope changes, because it is their project and they ultimately need to live with the results. The sponsor and the project team set expectations in the signed Project Definition. This is further clarified in the approved business requirements. These are the expectations that are in place. If people have requests for changes to these agreements, the sponsor needs to make the decision, based on the business value provided and the overall impact on the project in terms of cost, delivery time, or quality.

The sponsor also has the added advantage of organizational power. Although it is sometimes hard for the project team to say "no" to the client, the sponsor doesn't have that problem. Clients and end users usually work in the sponsor's organization. Since the sponsor is paying for the project, they are usually more concerned about it completing as promised within the budget and delivery date.

This change in expectations may be fine. The sponsor may ask your team to change the project scope, and also agree to the corresponding change in effort, cost, and scope. However, this is not a given—especially if the changes are very large or very small.

Jerry's sponsor is typical. She didn't have much patience for changes in scope resulting in marginal benefit. Small changes viewed as critical to the end users usually pale when viewed from the sponsor's perspective. On the other hand, if the change is important enough, the sponsor can provide the incremental budget and timeline required to complete the extra work. A side benefit of going to the sponsor is that after invoking the process once or twice, fewer scope change requests come up. People are much less likely to request changes without a very good business case if they realize the sponsor is actively evaluating all of them.

12 | Time for Tom to Take Some of His Own Medicine

I had been working as project management advisor for almost two full months now, and was interested in some feedback regarding my performance in this new role. My boss Wayne agreed to talk with some of his management peers to see if they had heard anything from their staff. Our meeting today was to discuss this feedback.

As I entered his office, Wayne opened his desk drawer and pulled out a brochure and photo and handed it to me, smiling. "Desert Oasis" was sprawled in fancy italic type across the front, with overlapping photos of a golf course, pool, and an elderly couple enjoying lunch.

"What's this?" I asked.

"Our new home," he replied. Wayne had already explained to me a few weeks ago how he and Elsie were going to move to a warmer climate this summer after his retirement, and how a friend had recommended the Desert Oasis resort. Apparently, he and Elsie had flown to Arizona last October and had toured the property. The tone of his voice told me he was excited.

Of course, I was happy for Wayne and his wife. But I knew it would also be tough seeing him retire and move away. In fact, after a few weeks of reflection, I was still somewhat in shock.

I reflected back on the conversation we had when Wayne broke the news about his retirement. "It was not an easy decision for us," Wayne had said. "But the winters seem to get colder every year, and we are not as young and limber as we used to be. When Elsie broke her leg slipping on the ice a few years back, we realized we needed to give more thought to our retirement plans."

"I understand. I am sure you guys have given this a tremendous amount of thought already. What are you going to do with the house?"

"We are thinking of putting it on the market next month. Elsie wants to hire a realtor, but I really don't know of anyone reputable. I don't suppose you know someone in the market for a new home?"

I had smiled at him and scratched my head, not giving it much thought. Then the light bulb went on. "You know what, Wayne? I may actually know someone who would be perfect for your house. Would you be willing to have a couple look at it this weekend?"

"Sure, not a problem," he had replied. "Who is it?"

"Jerry Ackerman."

Snapping out of my brief trance, I handed Wayne back his brochures. You never know how things will turn out, I thought. Wayne has a house for sale. Jerry is looking to buy a house. Maybe it will turn out to be a good match.

Wayne sat down in the big leather chair in front of his desk and gestured for me to take a seat. Putting the pictures back in the drawer, he pulled out a file folder and sat back contentedly.

"Well, I've got more good news, Tom," he started. "I spoke with four managers and all the feedback on your job performance was positive. Even your friend Jerry put together a decent Project Definition and workplan. In the past, he would have been a third of the way to disaster by now."

"That's great to hear," I said. "But was there any other feedback?"

"Not really. Just a lot of positive comments."

"Well, the feedback is nice, and I believe I am on the right track, but right now this is just 'feel-good' feedback. I guess it's time I start to collect some more meaningful data on the value I'm providing."

"Value?" Wayne questioned. "The feedback I received was that you have been providing a lot of value."

"Yes, and I appreciate the kind words. But the feedback is from fellow managers whom you have worked with for years. I hope their kind words are true, but I need to collect some more meaningful, quantitative comments on the value I am providing. I'm preaching the value of collecting metrics to the project managers whom I am working with. I guess I need to start taking some of my own medicine."

LESSON 12

COLLECT METRICS TO EVALUATE HOW WELL YOU (AND YOUR PROJECT) ARE PERFORMING

What if a company could not tell a shareholder its revenues or profits for the fiscal year? That company would have some serious problems to address. Likewise, if the same shareholder asked the company how its products were viewed in the marketplace, and it replied "good," that would not be very comforting for the shareholder either.

The preceding examples never happen, though, because companies collect metrics. They collect financial information on revenue and costs, and they collect data on how their products are perceived in the marketplace. For good or for bad, they typically know much of the information they need to run the business.

On a much smaller scale, a stakeholder might ask you how successful a recent project was, or how efficient a billing process is, or, in my case, what value I am providing with my coaching service. Those questions are usually harder to answer.

Many (probably most) companies have no idea whether they are getting value for the dollars they spend on projects, and they have only a vague idea about the success of individual projects. Defining and collecting an appropriate set of metrics is the only way to get quantitative and qualitative information, and is the only way to have the right information to make the decisions necessary to improve. Metrics must be collected to show the effectiveness and value of services being provided. Collecting metrics gives the information needed to improve processes, and gives results that show if expectations are being met.

My situation is a good example. I am providing a service to the organization, but I need to collect information to show the effectiveness and value of the service I provide to project managers. I cannot just rely on anecdotal comments from high-level managers. I need more facts and I am going to propose collecting metrics in the following areas:

- The number of project managers I am assisting, current month and year to date
- A satisfaction survey asking project managers about my service level and the value (or lack of value) I added to their projects
- Whether I kept my commitments, within the agreed upon time frame
- Any quantifiable numbers in terms of cost or time savings that can be attributed to my services

My job represents one small component of the entire organization. All teams should be collecting metrics. If an organization is not used to collecting metrics, the basic philosophy should be to just start collecting them—even if they turn out to be the wrong ones. It is important to start collecting some metrics, and to modify them over time if they don't provide indications of how effective and successful a project or the process is.

13 | Miles Learns an Important Lesson—for the Second Time!

My last appointment on the last day of February was with Miles O'Brien. Miles grew up in New York and was the oldest brother in a large Irish family. He had curly red hair and a white complexion, with bright green eyes. Miles was perhaps best known for his office attire on St. Patrick's Day. Every year he came to work dressed in a bright green suit and tie with a green top hat. I had been meeting with him on an ad-hoc basis to talk about his project to install a new release of the company's contract management application for the Purchasing Department. He came by my office around 4 p.m.

"How are you Miles?" I said as he came through the front door.

"I'm a little hungry, but otherwise things are great."

"I've got some leftover snacks from my lunch today. Would you like some crackers with peanut butter?"

"No thanks, Tom. I am actually on a diet. I need to lose about ten pounds before St. Patrick's Day or I won't be able to fit into my suit."

"In that case, we better get you some donuts and candy!" I replied with a chuckle.

"Oh, c'mon. Are you telling me you don't like my green suit?" Miles said with a smile. He told me he had tried it on several weeks ago, and had noticed the pants were a bit snug, which was why he needed to shed a few pounds. He was trying a low-carb diet in the hope of losing the weight quickly.

"Well, best of luck to you," I said after our conversation about his diet had run its course. "Why don't you fill me in on your project's status?"

"We were testing the new release of our package when we discovered that a small piece of the system contained custom code in need of a rewrite," he began. "This code was written a number of years ago by a contractor, and we forgot it would need to be upgraded separately."

"It's too bad you discovered the problem so late in the project," I said, "but at least you found it. I guess that says something about the value of good testing."

"I'm also glad we found it. It would have been pretty embarrassing if we hadn't. I found out this same problem occurred the last time the package was upgraded. Now I need to figure out how to make sure this is remembered the next time we do an upgrade."

"You're right," I said. "The accumulated knowledge of a project tends to exist only in the minds of the people who actually worked on it. You need to make sure this information is available for the next time your package gets upgraded."

LESSON 13

SAVE KNOWLEDGE FOR FUTURE PROJECTS, LEVERAGE KNOWLEDGE FROM PRIOR PROJECTS

So much organizational knowledge gets lost over time if no processes are designed to capture and exploit the information. This is the essence of knowledge management, which consists of the processes required to collect, organize, retrieve, share, and leverage the knowledge that exists throughout a company. Sometimes this knowledge is organizational in nature, but many times the knowledge is project based, and can be leveraged on subsequent projects.

Think about the knowledge accumulated during a project. It starts with the Project Definition and workplan, and continues through the Issues Log, business requirements, test plan, etc. On most projects, the project manager does not consider the future value of this information. In fact, in many cases, much of the knowledge will not be reused. However, on many projects, the knowledge learned, and written down, can be used again and again to save others time and effort.

Let's look at Miles's project to upgrade a financial software package. This software is going to be upgraded periodically, perhaps every other year or so. In this type of project, almost all information can be leveraged the next time a new release is installed. This includes the Project Definition, workplan, Issues Log, test plans, etc. However, taking advantage of the information requires forethought from both the old project manager and the new one.

First, before the project ends, time must be allocated to capture all of the relevant information and bundle it in one place for future use (don't zip all the information and place it in an obscure spot or on someone's local hard drive). Many teams have shared directories they utilize for project activity. A separate project folder should be established, and the material placed there. It should also be plainly named. If you have a document repository tool, make sure the proper keywords are entered to allow the documents to be easily found again. Saving and reusing the information allows the new project team to start off more quickly and avoid prior mistakes.

Much of the personal collective wisdom of the project can be captured during a formal project conclusion meeting. You can use this meeting to recap the project, discuss the things that went well and the things that could be improved, and look for any lessons learned. The results of this meeting can be documented and included in your overall project folder. (If you have a way to share this information with the rest of the organization, that would be even better.)

The second part is just as important. When a new project begins, the project manager must make a conscious effort to see what information already exists and can be leveraged on the project. Many organizations have processes in place to save information, but project managers don't always leverage that information, or even look for it, before embarking on a new initiative. Before starting a new project, always ask whether this problem (or a similar one) has been solved before. This is especially important when you have similar projects that need to be carried out periodically—such as a package upgrade.

Miles's project is a good example of this philosophy. He knows the contract management package will need to be upgraded periodically. He also recognizes that much of the work that occurs in one upgrade can be leveraged in the next upgrade. If the exact same people work on two upgrades in a row, the team might remember all of the details from one project to another. However, if different people are involved, perhaps an entirely new team, having the information from previous, similar projects available will be of great value to them. If Miles saves the appropriate information from his project, and if a new project manager reviews that information before starting the next upgrade, the project can save time, effort, and needless rework.

When the next upgrade project occurs, the team must remember to review and leverage the information from previous projects. The prior

Project Definition and project workplan can be leveraged for the subsequent project.

Your organization will gain the most value if it has a mechanism to capture and store information from all projects. In that way, all project managers can first look to see whether similar projects have been executed before. For instance, you may be asked to develop a Web reporting application for your client group. If your organization captures this information, you may be able to find similar Web reporting projects. You can review the workplans for these projects, their deliverables, the look and feel of their Web pages, etc. All this information may be helpful when defining and planning your project.

14

There's a Problem, but No One Tells Mike

March arrived in Dickens with a bang. A large cold front from the north created a snowstorm that deposited another three inches of fresh snow on the ground. Pam was very busy at work preparing for the men's college basketball conference tournament, which was being hosted by Northeast Illinois State, and I was busy painting our living room, replacing the kitchen tile, and helping people to manage projects at work.

My first meeting of the day on Monday was with Mike Miller, whose project was to install document management software in the Legal Department. Mike and I had driven to Chicago two weekends ago to catch a Bulls game, and we were quickly becoming good friends. After three months in my role as project management advisor, I began to realize I had very few friends to talk to about my own work. Most of my friends were colleagues from the office, and when we got together it was so they could talk to me about how work was going for them.

Mike, however, was always eager to listen, and always seemed to have something insightful and meaningful to say. He was also a big sports fan, and we could spend hours debating who the best NFL quarterback of all time was. He liked Joe Montana from the 49ers, but I preferred Johnny Unitas of the Baltimore Colts—old "Johnny Hightops."

When he arrived at my door, I was surprised to find him holding what appeared to be a gift. "It's for you," he said as he handed me the box. "Open it." I tore the paper from the box and opened it slowly, trying to add some dramatic flare. As I pushed the tissue paper aside, a smile formed across my face and I let out a loud laugh. It was a Joe Montana jersey.

"I thought you might get a kick out of that!" He said as he closed my office door.

"That's great Mike. Thanks a lot! Although I am not quite sure what to do with it!"

"Maybe you can regift it to me," Mike said as he took a seat and pulled out his project folder from his briefcase. *At the Bulls game, Mike mentioned his project was going very smoothly. I remember him saying his team had not yet encountered any major problems. In fact, they were scheduled to begin testing on the software last week.*

"Well Mike, you have almost completed the project without any hassle. But it sounds like something came up."

"You're right, Coach. I shouldn't have told you how smoothly things were going. Looks like I jinxed myself!"

"What's the trouble?"

"A problem was uncovered during our testing of the software," he began. *"It turns out the document management software doesn't interface well with one of our existing legacy systems, which is causing the legacy system to lock up on a regular basis."*

"That's a surprise," I replied. *"What kind of feedback have you been getting from the team members doing the testing?"*

"That's the frustrating part. I've been getting periodic updates from them and they've never mentioned this problem. The team said they thought they could resolve it on their own."

"Have you notified your clients?" I asked.

I could tell he was frustrated. "You are not going to believe this, but the clients already knew about the problem! Since they were helping to test the old system, they were the ones who discovered the problem to begin with."

"So, most of the team knew, except you," I concluded. *"Many technical people are natural problem solvers. They probably thought they could resolve this on their own. They also may have felt that raising an issue would have generated scrutiny of their work. They may not understand that issues management raises the visibility of a problem so it can be resolved quickly."*

"Two weeks ago, we probably could have resolved this and still met our project timeline. Now, the resolution may cause the end date to slip."

LESSON 14

ENSURE ISSUES MANAGEMENT IS EVERYONE'S RESPONSIBILITY

All projects encounter problems. In fact, for a larger project, there may be people talking to the project manager every day about one type of problem or another. These are not issues. Most are just typical problems requiring quick decisions to be made from one or more decent alternatives. At other times, there may not even be a problem involved. It may be a team member just doesn't know how to respond to a certain situation.

On the other hand, a formal issue is a problem that will impede the progress of the project because it cannot be entirely resolved by the project team. In other words, an issue is a big deal. It is a problem requiring special project management processes, including

- Proactive communication with the client, sponsor, team members, and other interested stakeholders
- Proactive and ongoing follow-up to ensure the issue is resolved as quickly as possible
- Special problem-solving techniques if the issue is not easy to understand or address

Sometimes when project team members hear about issues management, they think project management processes don't apply to them. After all, project management processes are for project managers, right? Wrong! To be successful, the entire team needs to understand they are all part of the process. One of their primary responsibilities is to raise issues when they see them. This responsibility isn't limited to the team either; business clients should also raise any issues they encounter. Raising an issue isn't a negative. It is a proactive way to identify a problem so the team can apply appropriate resources, find alternatives, and implement a resolution. On a large project, for instance, you may have a fairly rigorous process defined for managing issues. This entire process could look something like the following:

1. Solicit potential issues from any project stakeholders, including the project team, clients, sponsors, etc. An issue can be surfaced through verbal or written means, but it must be formally documented using an Issue Submission Form.

2. Enter the issue into the Issues Log.

3. Assign the issue to a project team member for investigation. (Project managers could assign it to themselves.) The team member will investigate options that are available to resolve the issue. For each option, he or she should also estimate the impact to the project in terms of budget, schedule, and scope.

4. The various alternatives and impact on schedule and budget are documented on the Issue Submission Form. Take the issue, alternatives, and project impact on the Issue Submission Form to the project sponsor and other appropriate stakeholders for a resolution.

5. If resolving the issue will involve changing the scope of the project, close the issue now and use the scope change management procedures instead to manage the resolution.

6. Document the resolution or course of action on the Issue Submission Form.

7. Document the issue resolution briefly on the Issues Log.

8. Make the appropriate adjustments to the work plan and project budget, if necessary.

9. If the resolution of an issue causes the budget, effort, or duration of the project to change, the current Project Definition should be updated.

10. Communicate issue status and resolutions to project team members and other appropriate stakeholders through the Manage Communication process, including the Project Status Report.

On Mike's project, team members discovered a problem and thought they could resolve it on their own. This is an admirable first step. You don't want to raise an issue for a problem the team can resolve itself. However, when the initial resolution attempts did not succeed, they should have raised this problem with Mike. Mike might have had other ideas to resolve the problem before it became an issue. If those ideas did not work, they could have raised a formal issue, which would have invoked a proactive issues management process. Since a third-party package was involved, the problem may not have been within the team's control to resolve. The team could have identified options to resolve the problem, suggested workarounds, or changed the project scope with the sponsor to make the issue irrelevant. Of course, all of those options are still available now. However, it may be too late to complete the project by the deadline date since the issue was not raised in a timely manner.

15

Ashley Is About to Gain an Hour a Week

I had just finished setting up another meeting with Jerry Ackerman when Ashley Parker walked into my office. We were going to lunch together to discuss her project, and she was a little early. There was a nice Italian restaurant, Mama Leoni's, a few miles south of our office, and we decided to go together in Ashley's SUV. That beats eating peanut butter and crackers at my desk any time.

Mama Leoni's was a family establishment built in the 1950s. The place had been renovated in the 1980s, but still contained the original leather booths from when it first opened. Anthony and Tina Leoni, the owners, still cooked on occasion, but Anthony, Jr., the Leoni's oldest son, now handled the day-to-day management of the restaurant. The building had withstood both fire and flood during its 30-year history, but had never closed for longer than two months.

It was March, and I had not seen Ashley since early January when she was struggling with a sponsor who had been reassigned during her project. I knew she had been able to gain agreement from her new sponsor on the work required for the next phase of her project, so we had not had reason to talk since. After ordering lunch, we got down to business.

"So, what's the latest Ashley? Everything okay with your new sponsor?"

"Oh yes, he's a great person. He's very professional and very thorough."

"Sounds great. How can I help you then?"

Ashley began discussing her project. She was having trouble with her status meetings, which she holds once a week with her clients and team members. She said she was having a hard time covering everything on the agenda in two hours.

"Your status meetings are two hours?" I asked in a surprised tone. "Tell me more. What does your agenda look like?"

Ashley went over the contents of the meeting matter-of-factly, counting off the items that she and her team discussed on her fingers—an update on the project and workplan, a discussion of the action items from the previous meetings, outstanding issues, and scope change requests. People could also add other small items to the agenda as needed.

"The agenda sounds good," I said. "Where do you think the meeting is breaking down?"

"I think the team tries to do too much problem solving during the meeting. We end up spending all of our time hashing and rehashing many of the same items from week to week. We also tend to get sidetracked, and it seems like we can never finish the meeting on time. Some members of the team think we need to lengthen the meetings to two-and-a-half or three hours."

"I have a better idea," I said quickly. "To get your meeting more focused and to better utilize everyone's time, don't add more time—reduce it instead. Cut the meeting back from two hours to one."

LESSON 15

SHORTEN LONG MEETINGS TO SHARPEN THE FOCUS

Status meetings are essential to ensure the project team and the client maintain healthy and open communication, and to ensure everyone's expectations are in sync. Even many of the streamlined, "light" project life-cycle methodologies rely on frequent, short team meetings to share information and status. A traditional status meeting usually includes representatives from the project team and the client organization—perhaps even the sponsor. Because many of the project decision makers are there, these meetings may seem like a good time to resolve open issues and action items.

In a large company like Mega Manufacturing, it can be difficult to get the right people focused and on the same page for decision making. If you can get all of them into a meeting, the temptation is to use that time to discuss and resolve problems. Unfortunately, this may result in people delaying their day-to-day decisions and, instead, bringing items to the status meeting for discussion and resolution. This diverts from the main purpose of the meeting and may result in a less functional day-to-day work environment.

On the surface, this might not seem too bad. After all, the right people are there. Why not engage in problem solving and decision making activities?

The problem, however, is that this is not the purpose of the status meeting. The purpose is to keep everyone up to date with what is going on, at a level where the information is of interest to all of the participants. In addition to a recap of project status, items such as scope change requests, issues, or new risks should be discussed, since they could impact everyone.

Bringing routine items to the status meeting for resolution will cause the meeting to break down—just the way Ashley's is doing. Small problems or questions that impact only a few people end up being discussed by a subset of the team. As the questions change, different people get engaged, but not everyone is involved. In a two-hour meeting, each person may only be actively participating for 30 to 45 minutes, and then wishing they were somewhere else for the remainder. Of course, not everyone can be actively engaged for the entire meeting, but 45 minutes out of a one-hour meeting is much better than 45 minutes out of a two-hour meeting.

As the project manager, Ashley can and should change the format and the agenda of the meeting. More than anyone else, she is responsible for making sure people's time is treated valuably. If she is not careful, people will start to complain that they are wasting their time, and they will begin to skip the meetings.

The good news is that Ashley seems to understand the meetings are not effective in their current format. She told me they are not able to cover all of the important business because they are spending too much time problem solving. Furthermore, her solution to extend the meeting seems appropriate, but it will cause even greater problems. Instead, she should use shorter meetings to force the team to be more focused. This will require better planning for the meeting, including communicating discussion items before the meeting starts.

It would be wrong to imply no decision making can occur at a status meeting. Decision making regarding issues, risks, and scope changes are perfectly acceptable. If everyone knows what topics will be covered ahead of time, they can discuss them rapidly and resolve them quickly. If it becomes clear a quick-and-easy resolution is not possible, then further discussion and decision making needs to be tabled and resolved offline.

The project manager normally acts as the meeting facilitator at a status meeting, and is responsible for making sure the meeting is relevant and does not get sidetracked. So, while Ashley is certainly frustrated by how the meetings are turning out, she is also responsible for controlling the agenda and making sure the discussion stays on track.

Ashley must be firm to keep the discussion from getting sidetracked. Again, these may be valuable conversations, but they are usually not appropriate for the status meeting. Items need to be identified, taken offline, and resolved in another forum. One option for her to consider is to reduce the formal status meeting to one hour, and keep the second hour open for any members who need further time for discussion. The people who were not impacted would be free to leave.

In general, longer meetings can leave numerous opportunities to wander. Short meetings force more focus on the areas needing to be covered.

16 Jade Resolves a Vendor Problem (Again and Again)

Jade Johnson was an older woman with curly black hair and a big nose. As far as I knew, she had never been married and still lived in an old house on Rutherford Street she bought more than 25 years ago. In my 10-plus years at Mega Manufacturing, I never knew anyone who had much knowledge about her, which was strange because she could tell you the life story, including the latest gossip, of everyone in the office.

It was literally spooky how much she knew about people. I will never forget the first day I met Jade. My wife and I had just moved to Dickens, and it was only my second day on the job. A colleague introduced us when we bumped into her by the vending machines in the break room. The first thing she said to me was, "So, you're the one who bought that house on Wood Ranch? Tell me, how do you and Pam like the place?"

I remember feeling an odd sensation in my stomach. I had never met this woman before, and she already knew where I lived and my wife's name. A few months later, I found out she went to lunch with a woman in Human Resources on my first day, which is how she found out some basic information. Still, I knew to be careful with what I said around her.

She stopped by my office early Tuesday morning to discuss an issue she was having on her project to add an accounts receivable interface with another bank.

"Hello, Tom. How are you today?" she said in a raspy voice.

"I'm doing fine. Sounds like you have a cold."

"Just getting over one actually. So, I hear you hooked up Jerry with the Morettis' place. I was surprised to find out Wayne is leaving Dickens. Tell me, where are he and his wife moving? Someplace south?"

I stared blankly into her face and shrugged my shoulders. I knew Wayne was going to Arizona, but I didn't know if it was common knowledge or not. If I told Jade, I knew it soon would be. She turned her head slightly to the right and squinted her eyes as she stared back at me for several seconds. Finally she sat down and turned her focus on to her project, which came as quite a relief to me.

Jade said her project required a number of changes to our interface files going to and coming from our main bank. She told me she was frustrated because the support staff at the bank was not available to help her team resolve a data transmission problem. My first question was whether she had tried escalating the issue at the bank.

"I guess that's the next step," she replied, tapping her long nails on my desk. "But they have really been difficult to work with. This is the third time I have escalated problems because their staff is unavailable. They must hate to hear from me by now."

I perked up. "This is interesting," I said. "Whenever I see a pattern, it makes me think a symptom of the problem is being resolved rather than the root cause. Why were the bank people unavailable?"

"They were allocated to other projects and were too busy to help us with our problems."

"Okay, but why were the bank people allocated to other work?"

"Well, I was told they have a huge workload. Their people all get fully allocated, which means it is hard for us to get help when we need it."

"Wait a minute," I said. "We are making a major change to our interface. We should be a part of their workload. Why aren't they allocating resources to us?"

Jade thought for a minute, and the nail tapping stopped as she realized what the answer was.

LESSON 16

IDENTIFY THE ROOT CAUSE OF PROBLEMS, ESPECIALLY IF THEY ARE REOCCURRING

As we saw earlier, issues are major problems that will impede the progress of a project, and are not totally within the ability of the project team to resolve. Every issue has a cause and every issue has an effect on the project. Some complex issues also have symptoms, which outwardly may look like a cause, but are not actually at the root-cause level. Symptoms are directly or indirectly related to the problem, but are not the cause of the problem itself. A symptom is actually more of an effect of the problem.

Sometimes, in the heat of the battle, the project manager sees the effect an issue has on the project, and looks quickly at the cause. In some cases, this first attempt at problem resolution actually addresses and fixes the cause. However, in other cases, the resolution only addresses a symptom, rather than the actual root cause. In many cases, resolving a symptom might, in fact, be good enough. The issue may go away and not return. However, if another similar issue arises later, it might mean a more funda-mental resolution is required.

Let's look again at Jade's problem in particular. Since her initiative requires major changes to the bank interface, she should have involved the bank IT staff in the planning process. However, she neglected to do so. If her team had not experienced any problems, Jade may have been more fortunate. However, the interface is complicated, and the team has run into a number of problems.

When her team hit the first problem, Jade realized the bank was not very responsive. However, she did not think the problem through to find the root cause of the response time problem. Her initial assumption was probably that they were not responsive because they did not have a good customer service mindset. But it turns out that was not the case. The way to get to the root cause is by asking a series of "why" questions. After ask-ing a series of "why" questions, Jade would have realized the bank support staff was unavailable because they were allocated to other projects and other clients. Jade did not communicate with the bank about what she was doing and about what her resource needs would be. Escalating the support issue at the bank only resolved the symptom at the time, which was that their staff was unavailable.

Jade resolved the particular problem she faced the first time, but she did not get to the root cause. Unfortunately, the problem did not go away for good. A little later a similar problem occurred with the bank's allocation of their staffing resources. Again, Jade resolved the particu-lar problem facing her team at that time by escalating the lack of sup-port staffing, but she did not resolve the root cause. Since this was the second time this problem occurred, Jade should have realized now that her first attempt at problem resolution did not resolve the root cause of this problem.

So, now she is bringing this to my attention. When I first heard of the prob-lem, I also jumped toward resolving the symptom by escalating the problem once again at the bank. However, when Jade said this was the third time the problem had occurred, I knew the root cause was not being addressed. The bank could not be responsive because their IT support staff was allocated to other customers. They were not allocated to Jade's project because she did not include them in her planning. Therefore, the bank did not know of her testing needs, and did not allocate any support resources to her project. Her best option now is to work with the support manager at the bank to get a person assigned to this project to help her team when they have problems.

17

Bailey Has Questions, but She Is Not Sure What They Are

My son Tim and I had been trying to plan a game of miniature golf after work for several days, but a persistent storm system over most of Illinois, bringing rain and sometimes strong winds, had so far prevented us from visiting the green felt links of our local Putt-Putt. I bought a special Mickey Mouse set of golf clubs for him last Christmas, and he seemed to enjoy swinging them in the back yard when the weather allowed, and in the basement when the weather didn't. The first week of April brought mild temperatures, and on the first sunny day I took Tim to play his first round of miniature golf. In my opinion, he putted fairly well for a youngster, although I wasn't sure if he enjoyed putting the ball into the hole as much as through the clown's nose or over the bumps and hills. I hoped he wouldn't be disappointed when he went to his first real golf course and found no windmill or concrete banks off of which to bounce his ball.

I was telling the story of our day on the miniature links to Marketing Manager Bailey Jenkins, who had been working with Ashley on the marketing information database project. Ashley and I had met a few times to discuss this project, but I had never met with Bailey before. She was really into meditation and I remember hearing nature CDs playing in her office when I would go over and visit with Ashley. When I asked Ashley about it, she said Bailey liked to meditate over her lunch hour.

"I tell you, Bailey, he might just be the next Arnold Palmer!" I said, finishing my story about Tim and miniature golfing.

Bailey flashed a smile that said she appreciated the story, but had no idea who Arnold Palmer was. I decided to put the "putter talk" aside and focus on project management.

"Bailey, it's always a pleasure for me to get to meet with our client managers. How can I help you?"

"The vice president of marketing has a lot of interest in making sure this marketing information database is implemented successfully," Bailey began.

"He has given us the necessary time, but he has also made it very clear he doesn't want to hear excuses if it goes in late. I think Ashley is doing a good job, especially given the confusion that occurred when our old vice president was transferred. I guess I'm nervous because of the high visibility. We cannot afford to fail."

I acknowledged Bailey's nervousness. "That's a natural feeling, Bailey. In fact, you and Ashley are both on the hook for the success of this project. If there are problems, the VP is going to look to you for answers. It won't be good enough to say Ashley was the project manager and it was her responsibility."

"That's exactly my point," Bailey agreed, taking a deep breath. "The VP put me in charge of this project to make sure we hit our project budget and deadline. However, most of my background is in the finance area. I reviewed the business requirements document created by the project team, but I don't have the expertise to evaluate the information. I want to be able to track the project adequately without getting involved in the details, but I don't know what questions to ask."

"It's hard for functional managers to be subject matter experts for every project in the organization," I said. "Your VP shouldn't expect you to have that level of knowledge. However, there are questions you can ask to make sure projects are proceeding as expected. These questions are part of your quality assurance role."

LESSON 17

USE QUALITY ASSURANCE TECHNIQUES TO VALIDATE THE STATUS OF A PROJECT

Managers want to delegate responsibility and autonomy to project managers, but they know they also retain a level of responsibility if the project is in trouble or fails. This level of accountability runs up to the sponsor as well. Projects that fail or overrun their budgets and deadlines also reflect poorly on the sponsor and, to varying degrees, on all other management stakeholders.

So, it is not surprising a sponsor, functional manager, or other high-level individual wants to understand the status of a project. Of course, they can read status reports, but they are pretty much taking the project manager's word on the status. In many cases, the status reports are so vague it is hard to know for sure what is going on.

So how do managers have a better idea as to the status of a project? They could review the documentation being prepared, but most managers are not experts in the business aspects of all the projects in their organization. If the work involves an IT development project, like Ashley's, they rarely have the expertise to understand the design documentation or the program code. Therefore, managers generally need to rely on quality assurance techniques.

The purpose of quality assurance is to ensure sound processes are used to create project deliverables (quality control is all about ensuring the deliverable itself is complete and correct). If managers cannot ensure that deliverables are of high quality based on their own experience, they must, at a minimum, feel the project team used a solid process to build the deliverable.

In this instance, Bailey is in the project sponsor role, which was delegated to her by the vice president, who is the executive sponsor. Bailey is in the Marketing Department. However, her real expertise is in finance, and the executive sponsor named her as the project sponsor to ensure the project met its budget and deadline commitments. It's not surprising then for her to be uncomfortable reviewing the business requirements document produced by the project team. Bailey cannot look at the business requirements document and know for sure whether the requirements are correct and complete.

Fortunately, she does not have to. She should put on her quality assurance hat instead. What she really needs to know is what the deliverable looks like, how it was created, who was involved in generating the requirements, who reviewed the document, and who approved the document. Depending on the answers, she may or may not feel comfortable with the deliverable. When she is performing quality assurance on the business requirements document, for instance, she can look for these signs to tell if more follow-up is needed.

Bad signs:

- The document is sloppy, poorly formatted, and hard to read.
- The requirements were generated by talking to one key user, plus the IT staff.
- The requirements were not formally approved.

Good signs:

- The document looks good, reads well, and follows a standard template format.
- The requirements were generated by getting all the key users and stakeholders together in a facilitated session for a full day.
- The document was reviewed and agreed to by all major users and stakeholders.

Quality assurance is not a one-time activity. It should be an ongoing part of your project. The manager of the project manager, and the sponsor, are the key individuals who should be performing a quality assurance check at the end of every phase, or during every major milestone.

If the project manager can explain and justify the process used to create the project deliverables, then there is a good likelihood the deliverables are acceptable. If the project is also within its budget, effort, and timeline estimates, then the manager or sponsor performing the quality assurance check should have confidence the project is on track. Similar questions regarding other deliverables can be asked as the project progresses through its life cycle.

18 The Project Nobody Wants

STEP 1 DEFINE THE WORK

"Hey Tom! How are you doing? Everything going okay?" I did not look up from my computer screen but immediately recognized Sam's voice. Sam Boyd, our Human Resources manager, was very "charismatic," to put it politely. It was mid-April, and Sam was completing our company recruiting for spring college graduates.

"I am doing just fine, thanks for asking. How are things in Human Resources?"

"Everything is going great. I just finished an interview with a young man by the name of Ron Klinger, who will be graduating from Northeast Illinois State next month. I was really impressed with him. He will graduate top of his class and he seems as sharp as a tack. I'd like to offer him a position here. Of course, I have to get an interview team set up. . . ."

Just then my phone rang. As a rule, the only time I interrupt a face-to-face discussion was when my boss called, but Sam motioned he had to leave anyway, so I waved good-bye and picked up the call. I was surprised to find Emma Flood on the other end.

Emma was the IT director in our Chicago office, and she wanted me to evaluate a project significantly over budget and long overdue to assess whether it was now on the right track. I agreed to offer my input, and arranged to "meet" via teleconference later in the day with two of the major project participants.

My first meeting was with Curtis Chapman, the project manager. He was desperately trying to establish a revised schedule and budget. I asked him what the project sponsor thought of the revised schedule, and he said he had exchanged e-mails with her and she seemed happy the project might finally be completed. I also asked whether the Project Definition document had been updated. He insisted there was really no need to update it, since the original assumptions, deliverables, scope, etc., were the same as before.

Then I talked with Jennifer Adams, the project sponsor. Jennifer was very unhappy with the whole project, and used the opportunity to vent her frustrations with the IT team. She held nothing back, saying it was doubtful the business value of the project would be achieved with the increased budget, and recent business changes made it questionable whether the original requirements were still valid. She said she would just be glad when the whole project was completed and behind her.

After the meetings, I collected my thoughts for a recommendation to Emma. When I spoke with her again, she was extremely curious as to what I thought of the project and its chance for future success.

I came right to the point. "Unless something changes very quickly, I think the project should be cancelled."

LESSON 18

CANCEL PROJECTS THAT LOSE BUSINESS SUPPORT, RELEVANCE, AND FOCUS

One of the advantages of being the project adviser is that I normally do not have any attachment to the projects I evaluate. Ownership, or partial ownership, of a project can sometimes cloud one's ability to make rational decisions.

It is generally understood if a project is approved, it must have inherent business value. In addition, the value must be such that the project is prioritized higher than other competing projects that are nominated but not approved. However, things change and nothing can be taken for granted when it comes to projects and the business value they provide. Market conditions change, project cost estimates change, and business priorities change. A project with great business value today might suddenly be irrelevant months, weeks, or even days later.

With that in mind, let's look at the project in the Chicago office. This project has already failed once, and is about to fail again. Sure, the project might be able to hit its revised timeline and budget—but what will the result be from a business perspective? The IT team, lead by Curtis, is determined to deliver the project as it was originally defined, even if the assumptions and expectations of the client have changed considerably. Curtis wants to pretend everything is okay, even though he must realize the inherent problems with the initiative at this point. To be charitable, he may just be hearing what he wants to hear from Jennifer, the project sponsor. He hears the sponsor saying she will be happy when the project is completed, but what she really wants is to get rid of the project. This is hardly the endorsement needed to proceed. The business situation has also changed, and the sponsor doubts the deliverables are even valid anymore.

Jennifer, the project sponsor, is not helping either. In fact, she may be more at fault here, since she knows the project is probably a failure at this point. The IT team could probably make the excuse they were continuing the project because the sponsor never told them to stop. This is a poor excuse, but it might provide them with a bit of cover if the project implodes.

Jennifer, on the other hand, doesn't have any excuses. She is willing to spend additional company resources on an effort she has lost confidence in, and from which she has already mentally checked out. She doubts the business value of the deliverables is there anymore. She doesn't want to make the mental investment to try to revise the objectives or the scope to make the deliverables relevant again. Furthermore, the fact the sponsor would be willing, even eager, to voice her displeasure with the project team is probably a sign the relationship between the sponsor and project manager has deteriorated beyond recovery.

Jennifer doesn't want to admit the work and money so far have been wasted. Since our company does not do a good job following up on whether projects achieve their business value, she probably feels the better alternative is to complete the project, gain some business value, and chalk the whole thing up to experience.

Both sides want to complete the project—but for the wrong reasons. The investment that has been made in this project may already be lost, and it would appear that further investment in the project in its current form would be a case of throwing even more good money away. Emma, the IT director, and the vice president of the client organization might make an assessment as to whether it makes sense to continue the project, but at this point that probably requires a reevaluation of the entire business value proposition. It's possible the project could continue with new sponsorship and a new project manager, but it would then probably need to restart with the planning and definition process to make sure it is still delivering something of value to the new sponsor. There is a lot working against this project. For now, the project should be placed on hold, or simply cancelled. Sometimes it's better not to complete a project. This is one of those times.

19 Jade Discovers a "Baby" Risk on Her Project

I received an e-mail from Jade Johnson on April 30 asking if she could come by and see me. Jade's team was making a number of changes to our interface files going to and coming from our main bank. I told her she could come by in the afternoon. She was a little vague and explained her problem was not yet "official," but she would contact me in a few days. I was not sure what she meant, but she said she would explain later.

Jade called me this morning to schedule an afternoon meeting, and I had to admit she had aroused my curiosity. She arrived five minutes early for our appointment, and since I was already in my office, I asked her to come in.

"How are you today, Jade?"

"I am fine, Tom. How are you?"

"Things are great, thanks for asking. Tell me, though, Jade, what's going on with your project? You mentioned last week you had a problem, but it was not an 'official' problem. Can I assume it is now?"

"Sorry for the confusion, Tom. Yes, it is a problem now. You see, last week I was speaking to one of our team members and she told me Kristen in the Finance Department is pregnant! She then told me it was a secret for now and I should not mention it to anyone. Of course, this causes a big problem for us, but I could not address it until she officially announced it. I got an e-mail from Kristen this morning letting me know about her pregnancy, so now I guess the cat's out of the bag."

Jade explained about how many of the activities in the project plan relied on Kristen's expertise. She was going to be instrumental in the success of the project, since she had provided the business expertise and leadership for setting up the bank interfaces a few years ago. Jade wanted to rely on Kristen again, but Kristen's e-mail mentioned she was three months pregnant and would be taking an extended leave from work when the baby was born.

"Here is my dilemma," Jade said. "If we are lucky, we will have the project done by the time Kristen has her baby. But if the baby comes early or if the project is delayed, we could be in trouble."

I asked Jade how she planned to account for this.

"Well, I called you just to be sure," she said. "I think this is definitely an issue. You know what you always say—'issues are problems.'"

"Well, I'm glad you remember about issues," I said. "But this situation is not yet a problem. It is a potential problem. You should identify it and manage it as a project risk."

LESSON 19

USE RISK MANAGEMENT TO RESPOND TO PROBLEMS BEFORE THEY OCCUR

Issues and risks are related but not the same. Issues are large problems present today that will impede the project if left unresolved. They must be focused on and resolved quickly. You have no other choice. By its nature, issues management is a reactive project management process, since you do not invoke it until the issue has already arisen.

On the other hand, risks are future conditions or circumstances outside the control of the project team that will have an adverse impact on the project should they occur. In other words, an issue is a current problem that must be dealt with, whereas a risk is a potential future problem. The good thing about a risk is you have some time to deal with the threat. Risk management is the process of identifying, analyzing, responding to, and controlling project risks. Risk management is a proactive project management process, since you are trying to deal with potential future events.

Risk management is not a one-time process. You should always identify risks at the beginning of the project during the up-front definition process, but you should also periodically look at remaining work to identify any new risks. This evaluation can take place on a periodic basis (e.g., monthly) or on project milestones.

Such is the case with Jade's project. When the project was started, there was no mention of the risk associated with losing Kristen, the strongest and most experienced analyst in the client organization. This makes sense. Although there was a very small chance any individual person might leave a project team, there was no reason to elevate this to a risk level needing to be identified and controlled.

However, events have changed, and now there is a definite possibility that Kristen's expertise will not be available to the project team before the project completes. Kristen is still on the project today, so there is no issue to be dealt with immediately. There is a potential problem in the future, but notice it is not a certainty. In fact, it is a certainty that Kristen will be taking maternity leave, but in all likelihood the project will be over by then, or at least be past a point where Kristen's expertise is critical. However, that result cannot be taken for granted, hence the need to identify this as a project risk.

Jade must put a risk plan in place to respond to this potential problem. A common objective of the risk plan is mitigation, which means you try to ensure the risk event does not occur (there are other options as well, which will be addressed in another lesson). Looking at Jade's project, the timing of the new baby's arrival cannot be controlled, so eliminating the risk event is not an option. However, since Jade has identified this risk early, she has plenty of time to control the impact of the event to ensure the project can still be completed successfully. Potential options for Jade to consider include

- Accelerating the work Kristen needs to perform so there is a good likelihood it will be completed before she leaves

- Cross-training a replacement in the client organization who can take over from Kristen if she has to leave early

- Replacing Kristen altogether with another resource, while still utilizing her as a backup and a mentor for her replacement

Since Jade has time, this project risk will likely be resolved before there is an impact on the project. That is the nature of risks. Since they are future events, you have at least some time to deal with them before they occur. There may not be a good way to resolve the risk, but at least you have some time to attempt a risk response.

20

Jerry Has a Small Problem (Unfortunately in Front of the CIO)

Jerry called me to set up an afternoon meeting on May 1. I invited him to lunch, but he asked for a raincheck as his schedule was crazy. Jerry and I exchanged e-mails frequently, and he mentioned last week he and his wife were getting excited about moving into Wayne's house. The Morettis were moving to Arizona in July, and planned to leave Illinois during the last week of June. Jerry was already beginning to pack up the apartment, preparing to move in shortly after the Morettis moved out. Jerry had filled out the necessary paperwork to take over ownership of the Morettis' home, and had already secured the mortgage from the bank. I volunteered to help him move when the time came, and he gladly accepted.

Jerry was also approaching a significant milestone at Mega Manufacturing, or at least I thought it was significant. He was in the final week or two of his project to upgrade the phone mail system, and most of the changes had already been implemented. He had not had a major problem pop up for almost a month, and I could tell his confidence was sky-high as he witnessed the fruits of his labor. At least it was sky-high before last Friday.

Jerry arrived on time for our meeting and began filling me in on the problem he had encountered. He was wearing a blue suit with a red-and-yellow striped tie.

"Why the fancy suit, Jerry? Do you have a job interview today?" I knew the joke was lame, but it's always the first thing I think of when I see someone in a suit.

"No, actually Barbara and I are celebrating our anniversary today. I am taking her to a pricey restaurant for dinner right after work."

"That's great. Happy anniversary!" I said, standing up to shake his hand. He filled me in on his dinner plans before getting down to business.

"The CIO asked us to give him a demo of the new voicemail software," he started. *"This should not have been a problem, but when we went to his office, wouldn't you know it—the system didn't work right! We had to come back half an hour later to finish the demonstration. He liked the new system, but I'm not sure he is totally confident in our ability to install it."*

"Sounds embarrassing," I said. *"What went wrong?"*

"We're trying to get additional people trained on how to install the software," he replied. *"Unfortunately, we assigned one of our newer people to work on the CIO setup, and he missed one of the steps. Maybe he cannot be trusted to do the upgrade. We may have to remove him from the project."*

"Whoa," I cautioned. *"You have thousands of phones to upgrade. I think you are going to need all the help you can get. Tell me, what procedures are in place to help these new technicians?"*

Jerry thought carefully for a minute. "The techs are supposed to understand phones and the voicemail software. We spent time showing each person what needed to be done for the upgrade, and we assumed they were skilled enough and professional enough to do the job."

I started to see a problem with the team's quality process. "You know, you are going to have to upgrade dozens of phone switches and thousands of phones for this project. It seems to me that even if your team is very diligent, there is a good chance problems will crop up on some of the installations. High-quality projects are only partially the result of good people. They are also the result of having good quality processes. When quality problems like this surface, don't blame your people—fix your processes instead."

LESSON 20

FOCUS YOUR QUALITY MANAGEMENT ON PROCESSES, NOT PEOPLE

If people always produced high-quality results, there would be no need for quality management. However, even the best people make mistakes, including project managers! Sometimes they don't even know it. For instance, quality problems can result from misunderstandings or from defects in raw materials. In other words, you may be doing everything right as far as you know, and problems can still occur.

One core project management responsibility is to manage the overall quality of the deliverables produced. Creating a quality plan that identifies quality control activities and quality assurance activities is one aspect of managing the overall quality.

Quality control activities validate the specific quality of the deliverables, usually after the fact. For instance, software testing a computer program is a quality control activity.

Quality assurance activities ensure the processes utilized in the project are of high quality, and will result in quality deliverables. This could include client review and approval of deliverables.

A project team cannot deliver consistent, high-quality products without good processes in place. Of course, you want to have good, motivated people as well. But, if you put good people into a complex, chaotic situation without good processes or guidelines, they are bound to struggle as well.

Quality processes must be scaled to the size, complexity, and importance of the project. Small projects have simple, basic quality checks built into the workplan. Larger projects have good overall quality processes in place, as well as metrics to determine the level of quality being produced. The team should monitor the quality metrics and improve the overall work processes when possible.

You will notice that nothing described so far focuses on people. There was no mention of hiring only the best people, or reassigning people who make mistakes. If good processes are in place, and if people work according to those processes, then everything should be fine. In a quality organization, you don't blame people when things go wrong. People are bound to make mistakes. It is in our nature.

Let's go back and look at Jerry's project. Jerry's frustration with a team member's performance is misplaced. Sure, it hurt when the upgrade process failed for the CIO. But other employees are bound to face similar problems as the upgrade is rolled out. What is he going to do—replace every team member who makes a mistake? Instead, Jerry needs to focus on processes. As it is organized now, Jerry's project plan is asking his team members to perform their work with very little structure and support, while he hopes nothing will go wrong. That's not a recipe for success. Instead, he should create a quality process to ensure everyone will be successful. This process could include providing better initial training, creating written procedures or checklists, pairing up new members with more experienced people, and having a second person perform quick random checks of the phones as they are converted. The first key to quality management is having processes in place to ensure things are correct the first time.

21

I'm Eating a Burrito, Jeff's Eating His Contingency

May 5 was a fun day for the employees at Mega Manufacturing. The company always paid for a nice Cinco de Mayo luncheon, and brought in catered food from Tico Taco, one of the few Mexican restaurants in Dickens. For most people, the annual party provided a nice opportunity to get outside and enjoy socializing with colleagues in an open environment. It was also always nice to see Dennis Lucas, our CEO, wearing a sombrero. Dennis was in his 60s and wore small, round glasses on his tiny head. He also had a bald head, which allowed the sombrero to slide over his ears to the top of his glasses.

I had just arrived at the party and was enjoying a burrito with extra jalapeños when Jeff Erickson came over to say hello. Jeff had just returned from a week's vacation in the Bahamas, which he had won from a radio station after correctly identifying a montage of songs from the 1980s. He had a dark tan and a bright smile on his face.

"I take it the vacation went well," I said as I shook his hand.

"It was incredible, Tom, and so relaxing. My wife and I tanned on the beach every day and just listened to the waves crashing as we sipped piña coladas. I feel like a new man!"

Jeff and I had worked a lot together when I was still with the IT department, but I had not spoken to him since the New Year's Eve party. He was a tall guy with a big body frame. He liked to lift weights and frequently worked out at the gym over his lunch hour. He was not the typical computer nerd, which is probably why we got along so well when we worked together.

"Say, Tom, I wonder if I could ask your opinion on a problem I am having with a project?"

"Sure Jeff. What's going on?"

Jeff gave me a quick summary of his project involving the installation of manufacturing software for one of his clients. He spoke about his Project

Definition and the progress his team had made so far on the project, and also mentioned it was the fourth time he had installed this software at one of our plants.

"The installation process for this software is similar at each plant, but each plant has its own unique needs as well. For instance, the plant manager in our current installation has requested we implement a custom inventory management module the other plants do not need."

"A custom module?" I asked in surprise. "I thought you said you were only going to implement base package functionality. If there is a new business need, I hope you are invoking scope change management."

"I talked to the client about scope change," he replied. "But they know our cost estimate includes a 15 percent contingency. They approved the additional contingency, so they thought we could use that funding for this new work."

"Tell me, why did you include the 15 percent estimating contingency?"

"The contingency covered a couple of unknowns," Jeff explained. "I am the only one on the team who has done this kind of project before; and it may take some time to get the rest of my team up to speed. We are also installing a newer release of the package than was installed at the other plants. The other packages are all an older release."

"Those sound like valid reasons to add contingency," I concluded. "What will happen if your people need extra time with the learning curve or the new software has some unexpected glitches, but you have used up your contingency on work outside of scope?"

Jeff was getting the idea. "I guess the project will be over budget. Then I will look like a bad project manager, even though I thought I was being client focused."

LESSON 21

DON'T USE YOUR ESTIMATING CONTINGENCY FOR SCOPE CHANGES

The only time you know for sure what a project will cost and how long it will last is after the work is completed. By its very nature, estimating is a guess. Of course, by using proper estimating techniques, you can make it a very close guess. However, there is always some degree of uncertainty in an estimate.

One of the steps in the estimating process is to add contingency to reflect the level of uncertainty associated with the estimate. If your estimate is at a high level, the contingency could be plus or minus 50 percent or more. However, even if most of the facts are known, a contingency of plus or minus 10 percent would not be unreasonable. This contingency can apply to effort, cost, and the project deadline.

When you place a contingency in the project, everyone should understand it is there to recognize the estimating uncertainty. However, once the estimate is approved, there may be pressure to use the contingency budget to absorb additional requirements instead. Your client may start to think of the contingency as "extra money" to be spent as needed. Although it is tempting to use the contingency when new functionality is requested, the project manager must ensure the estimating contingency is used as intended.

Jeff's project has just begun, and there is already a request to use the contingency. Using the contingency for this additional requirement would open the project up to two risks. First, the project could go over budget if the uncertainties associated with the original estimate come true. The budget contingency is there in case activities take longer than anticipated, or in case the original estimate left out work that should clearly have been within scope. If you use the contingency for extra work outside of scope, you will have nothing (or less) left over for estimating errors. As Jeff realizes, he will then be seen as a poor manager (or a poor estimator) even though he may think he is being client focused right now by agreeing to his client's request.

Second, by skipping the scope change process, Jeff is denying the sponsor an opportunity to make a decision as to whether the requested change is justified from a cost/benefit perspective. Instead, he and the plant manager are making the decision themselves. Although the plant manager is a key stakeholder, he is not the person funding this entire project.

Jeff's best option now is to push the request through the scope change process and let the sponsor determine if it is worth the incremental time and cost to the project. If so, the project budget and timeline should be increased to cover the work.

The client should not worry that the contingency budget will be wasted. As the project progresses, portions of the estimating contingency can be released back to the client if the project is trending on or ahead of schedule. Any money remaining from the estimating contingency at the end of the project can be returned to the business client (or retained as additional project profit from an external customer).

22

Communication Is King on Reyna's Project

The burritos, tortilla chips, and guacamole left a heavy feeling in my stomach, so I decided to skip the remainder of the party and take a walk. There was a small wine shop about a block south of the Mega Manufacturing building, and I figured a quick walk there and back would do me good. Of course, one cannot just walk to a wine shop without taking a quick look around, so I factored a quick stop into my schedule as well. I figured I could make it there and back in 30 minutes, which was when the Cinco de Mayo party was scheduled to end.

The Wine Depot was owned by Brent Bonds, and it carried a nice variety of "everyday" wines, as well as a few hard-to-find gems. I was not a wine snob, but Pam and I enjoyed a bottle every now and again. I liked the place because Brent was very knowledgeable and always made good recommendations. A tiny bell atop the door rang as I entered, and Brent poked his head over the top row of bottles in the Merlot section to say hello.

I browsed amongst the wines on display in the store for a few minutes, and decided to buy a bottle of Columbia Crest Grand Estates Chardonnay on sale for $11.99. Pam mentioned she was making fish for dinner, and Brent said the chardonnay would go perfectly with the meal. At $12, I decided to take his word for it.

When I returned to my office, I was surprised to find Reyna Andersen waiting outside my door. Reyna and I had spoken only occasionally since Wayne introduced us, and she explained she had just come from a meeting with her sponsor. Going into the meeting, she was working on a straightforward project to implement a customer relationship management (CRM) package. After the meeting, however, the project had become much more complex, and she immediately wanted to talk to me about it. I tucked my bottle of wine into my workbag and asked Reyna to come in and sit down.

"My sponsor just informed me their division has reorganized," she began. "We need to implement this CRM package in our Canadian and Mexican operations as well."

"Wow, that's a major change!" I replied. "I'll bet you want to talk to me about scope change management."

"Actually, I don't," she replied. "I explained to the sponsor her request was way outside the scope we agreed to. She agreed and asked us to come up with a new estimated budget and end date. My biggest concern is being able to communicate and work successfully in the other countries. I have never been to either country, and I don't know what to expect."

"I think I would have the same concerns," I agreed. "There are no specific problems right now, but when you are working internationally, communication cannot be taken for granted. The good news is the change in scope has come before the project has gone too far. You should have time to deal with it."

"Exactly!" Reyna replied. "But I don't know what to do next. This CRM initiative requires a culture change for the sales staff. Communication was already critical, and now it is even more so. I need to call a team meeting to try to get a handle on the communication needs, and work with my team to plan how we can successfully operate in these different cultures."

"Bingo!" I said approvingly. "You have solved your own problem."

LESSON 22

DEVELOP A COMMUNICATION PLAN TO ADDRESS COMPLEX COMMUNICATION REQUIREMENTS

Culture change refers to changing the way people perform their jobs. Implementing a culture change initiative in one organization requires a multifaceted communication strategy to be successful. Add a widely dispersed client base, including stakeholders in foreign countries, and it can really be scary.

All the potential problems can usually be overcome with enough planning and proactive project management. Risk management can be invoked to address these potential problems, but the key item for resolving the risk is a formal Communication Plan. Creating a Communication Plan involves following a simple process:

1. Identify the key clients, users, stakeholders, etc.
2. Determine their communication needs.
3. Brainstorm ways to fulfill the communication needs. This is an opportunity to be creative.

   The communication options will fit into three main categories:

   - Mandatory: This generally includes project status reports, legal requirements, financial reporting, etc. This information is pushed out to the recipients.

   - Informational: This includes information people want to know, or information that the project team wants to provide for them. This information is usually made available for people to read, but requires them to take the initiative, or pull the communication. An example is having a project Web site.

   - Marketing: These activities help to build buy-in and to add enthusiasm for the project and its deliverables. This type of information is pushed out to the appropriate people. Examples include newsletters, success stories, project posters, speaking at department meetings, etc.

4. Evaluate the options in step 3 to determine which provide the most value at the least cost and impact to the project, and cover all of the stakeholders to some degree. Since you can't do everything, these are the communication activities to start with.

5. Fill in the communication details and move to the project workplan. This includes the timing of the various communications, the effort required, dependencies, and who is responsible.

Even though Reyna has not had responsibility for an international project, others in the company have. She needs to speak to them to determine the type of communication and interaction that works best with the Canadian and Mexican staff. Once she has a good communication process in place, she should monitor it to ensure people are getting the information they need. If not, the plan should be modified as appropriate throughout the project. This could mean including some of the additional communication activities identified earlier, or coming up with new communication ideas based on the experience of the project so far.

Good proactive communication is vital in a culture change initiative like this. It is not the only area Reyna must address, but it is the foundation upon which all other incentives will be built.

23

Ron, the New Guy, Learns About Project Management Scalability

Sam in Human Resources set up a meeting with me for the afternoon of May 28 with a new employee. It was Ron Klinger, the recent graduate Sam had mentioned to me last month. He had accepted our offer last month, and had only been on the job for about a week. The two of them came by my office around 2 p.m., and Sam introduced us.

"Tom Mochal, this is Ron Klinger," he said. "Ron just graduated from Northeast Illinois State and started with us last week." Ron looked young. Did I look that young when I graduated college? He must have been 22 or 23, and his overall look was crisp and professional. I didn't know how smart or skilled he was, but he looked like a businessman. I was impressed.

"It is a pleasure meeting you," I replied. "Actually, I remember Sam speaking briefly about you after your initial company interviews. If I remember correctly, you were top of your class."

"That's right," Ron said with pride. "I am really anxious to get started and prove myself."

"That's actually why I brought Ron by today," Sam interjected. "He is starting a new project and I wanted you to give him some advice on how best to proceed."

Surprisingly, Sam said little else and left shortly thereafter, giving Ron and me some time to discuss his assignment. He was responsible for creating a real-time equipment utilization report for a manufacturing division client. Actually, I was a little concerned. It was not unusual to give new people responsibility, but to ask Ron to lead a project as his first assignment seemed aggressive. Perhaps he had some prior experience managing projects at school.

"Tom," Ron began, "I know you have a standard Project Definition document and I wanted some help developing it for the first time. I have a good idea what the objectives and scope are, but I'm not sure about a couple of the other sections like risk, budget, and the overall approach."

"Great," I replied. "We can walk through the major risks, and I can also give you a risk template for you to complete on your own."

"Good. I am also not sure exactly how we do budgeting here, so I will need some help going over my estimate and determining what the cost will be."

The kid sure seems to be asking the right questions, *I thought. "Not a problem. I can give you an overview of how we do budgeting, and then you can confirm some of the details with your manager."*

"I think the only other area I am not sure about is the project approach section. I just need more clarity on what you expect to see there."

"That section can be a little tricky, but by the time you get your initial workplan laid out, you should have the information you need to complete the approach. How many people will be working with you on this project?"

Ron was a little surprised. "Well, right now I am the only one identified," he said.

Now it was my turn to be surprised. "Really? You are going to put the whole application together yourself?"

"Yes. There will just be one new online screen to create," Ron said.

I was beginning to get the picture. "Ron, how much effort are you estimating it will take to complete this work?"

"I should be able to complete it in about 80 hours," Ron said.

I was now able to shift gears and start down a new line of questioning. The rest of our conversation was focused on gathering only the information Ron needed to define a small enhancement project.

LESSON 23

SCALE YOUR PROJECT MANAGEMENT PROCESSES BASED ON THE SIZE OF THE PROJECT

Much of the work done in a company can be structured and organized as a project. In turn, all projects need to be managed. However, the process (or methodology) used to manage the work needs to scale up and down, depending on the size of the work effort.

For instance, large projects should have a formal definition and planning phase, as well as rigorous processes for managing and controlling the work. In fact, it would not be unusual for a very large project of 10,000 hours to require 1,500 hours of project management time. Medium-sized projects still require some level of planning and some processes for managing and controlling the work. For instance, on a 1,000-hour project, only

150 hours of project management time might be needed. Note the percentage is the same (15 percent), but the total hours are down considerably. The same rigorous project management processes for a 10,000-hour project would not be needed for a 1,000-hour project.

How about a small project? A person may not need much "formal" planning or managing at all if the project is small enough. The planning and managing could probably be done in the person's head as he or she goes. For instance, a 10-hour project (such as a small enhancement) may only need an hour of project management. This hour is not spent on formal project management procedures, but might include completing a simple work authorization form, mapping a plan of attack in your head and some simple communication with stakeholders.

Let's look again at Ron's project. I give him credit for being eager to follow project management processes, but he is not scaling the processes appropriately. It doesn't make sense to spend 10 hours to write a Project Definition document for a project requiring only 80 hours of effort. He doesn't need to define formal objectives, scope, or approach. Those concepts have less meaning for small work efforts. He doesn't need to follow formal project management procedures. The chances of running into a major scope change or having to manage a risk are very small on a project of this size.

Fortunately, our department has some processes and forms that reinforce the scalable nature of the work. For instance, we have a one-page document called a Service Request form, which is used to define small enhancements and other minor initiatives. Once I realized the work effort was small, I made Ron aware of this form and we spent the rest of our meeting going over the handful of items on this form. All changes to production applications should be documented and approved by the client manager responsible for that application. The Service Request Form allows the client manager to see the request and the estimated effort. They can then approve the change request as well as prioritize the work against all of the other service requests that might be under consideration at any given time.

The lesson for Ron is to make sure he does not blindly follow a methodology. Our organization has some standards and requirements for all projects, and of course, these should be followed. He can determine which other project management processes make the most sense for his project and add them to the workplan as well.

24 Brian Can't Plan First, but He Still Needs to Plan

Brian White was a project manager in his early 30s who had a reputation for being very easygoing and was extremely well-liked. A talented musician, he often played his guitar around town at open microphone nights in bars or coffee shops. He would put up fliers in the break rooms advertising these events, and there were always at least a few employees who would show up to cheer him on. I had never seen him perform, but I had heard he played a mellow set, including several cover songs from Simon and Garfunkel. Given his relatively young age, I was surprised to find out about his affinity for the "Bridge over Troubled Water" duo. A few weeks ago, I helped Brian put together an estimate for a wireless Internet project for Mega Manufacturing's R&D department. He had good news and bad news when I met with him for the second time.

"The estimate we worked on a few weeks ago has been accepted!" he said, smiling broadly. "However, the timeline for completing the project has been shortened. My manager said a couple of other business units are interested in the new technology, and they want this proof-of-concept project completed as soon as possible."

"Well I guess that's good news," I agreed. "Do you need help with the Project Definition? I think the project is small enough that we can use the abbreviated version."

"I agree the definition document is normally important," Brian said. "But we are already past the planning process. Based on our earlier deadline date, we are already starting the work."

I could foresee potential problems if Brian went forward like this. "Really?" I questioned. "What are your deliverables? What is your approach? Where is your timeline? What is in scope and out of scope?"

Brian could only give me partial answers, which made me even more nervous. I think his early excitement made him think he could get by without *a plan. The shortened deadline then got him thinking he did not have time for the planning.*

"It sounds like you only have a vague idea of what you are going to do and what the expectations are," I pointed out. "One of the purposes of definition and planning is to ensure you have an agreement with your sponsor on what is expected. Otherwise, you will only be able to define your plans and deliverables after you have started the project and by then it will be too late to meet your deadline.

"But what about that deadline?" Brian insisted. "We've got to start now if we want to get the work done on time."

"Planning is not a luxury you do only if you have time," I countered. "Planning is a part of the project. If you have a choice, it's better to define and plan the project first, and then execute the plan. However, sometimes you have to start the project immediately and plan the work while some of it is already in progress."

LESSON 24

DEFINE AND PLAN THE PROJECT, EVEN IF YOU HAVE TO START THE WORK AT THE SAME TIME

Project managers often need to start working on a project before the planning is complete. This could be because of time pressure, like Brian's project, or it could be caused by the project team being assigned before the planning is completed. In the latter case, the project manager would need to have work available to keep the team members busy. These are not optimal situations, but they happen all the time.

When project execution starts early, there is a tendency to think you can get by without the up-front definition and planning. Since the planning normally occurs first, it may seem as if the time for planning has passed and cannot be recovered. However, this is not the case. If you don't plan, you won't know what your deliverables are, what your scope is, or what the workplan looks like. Even if you think you know the answers, you will not have confirmed that they are correct with your sponsor to make sure you are all on the same page.

It is possible to successfully define and plan the work after the project work has started. The trick is to assign resources to activities you are confident will need to be done in any case. For instance, most projects have some up-front analysis work. You can assign resources to work on the analysis while you are completing the planning. The ability to assign and manage work, while you are also performing the initial planning, is time consuming and requires the project manager to be well organized, disciplined, and able to multitask. It's hard work, which is another reason why many project managers skip it if the project has already started.

At some point, the definition and planning work will be completed. The project manager now has an agreement with the sponsor on what needs to be done, and a workplan that shows how to get the work done. The project manager can then confirm what work has been completed so far, and can make sure nothing critical has been missed. You should also check whether you have assigned unnecessary work. You may have assigned and completed some unnecessary work, but that is the tradeoff for having to start the work early. Hopefully, any wasted work effort will be made up for by an increased ability to deliver to an early deadline. On a project like this, the deadline date is normally more important than the effort and cost, and your sponsor is usually willing to be a little inefficient to achieve the deadline date.

The reward of this definition and planning is the ability to manage the rest of the project proactively.

The alternative scenario is that the project work gets too far ahead of your embryonic schedule and the definition and planning process never catches up. The risk to the project of skipping the definition and planning includes

- An inaccurate workplan, resulting in missed activities or extra, unnecessary activities throughout the project
- A loose understanding of scope, resulting in small and large scope changes
- Deliverables that do not meet the client's expectations
- An uncertainty of the project risks and how to respond to them

In this specific project, I would not recommend that Brian stops everything to complete the definition and the planning first. However, he still needs to proceed with the planning, along with the project execution. In the short-term, he can identify work that must be done, regardless of the outcome of the planning process, and assign team members to this work. Brian should also continue to plan out the work and get approval and agreement on what the project will do, what the deliverables are, etc. Based on the size of his project, he can define the work by completing an Abbreviated Project Definition. When the Abbreviated Project Definition and workplan are completed, he can synchronize the plan with the work already done and proactively manage the rest of the project from there.

25

Ashley Finds Not All Critical Path Activities Are "Critical"

The majority of my work involved meeting with people and helping them through one or two particular project problems. I rarely had a chance to meet with someone regularly and help them to complete their project from start to finish. That was a big reason why Jerry and I had become very comfortable working with each other. Meeting with him regularly had made me feel like a part of the team and had allowed me to see not only the progression of the project, but also his professional progression as he learned more and more about being a better project manager.

Another person I had helped frequently—although not as often as Jerry—was Ashley Parker. It was the middle of June; her team had just completed work on the new marketing information database, and she invited me to attend their project conclusion meeting. The project completed three weeks behind schedule and was over budget by 15 percent. These are not terrible numbers, but an interesting discussion ensued as to the causes of these overruns and how they could have been avoided. Ashley began the meeting by congratulating the team on a job well done.

"First off, my sincerest thanks to all of you for working so hard on this project. You all did a wonderful job, and you should feel proud of your work and our accomplishment. Of course, as with any project, we did encounter a few problems. That's the purpose for our meeting this morning. Knowing what we know today, what could we have done differently on the project to hit our deadline and budget?"

Chris, one of the database administrators, spoke up. "For the first half of the project, we seemed to have everything going according to the schedule. But some of the design decisions we made up front didn't pan out like we hoped, and caused us rework delays later on."

"That's a good point," Ashley noted. "The design work is critical on a project deploying new technology. For a project like this, that type of work should have been on the critical path."

"I think we also lost some focus toward the middle of the project," Diane contributed. "As we started to create the physical database, we were heading into the holiday season. I think things started to slip at that point."

"You're right," Ashley agreed, nodding. "It's imperative to maintain work focus around the holidays. If I had to do it again, I would have added some of those activities to the critical path as well."

"Another thing I noticed," Ashley continued diplomatically, "was I had problems understanding some aspects of the project management tool we were using. About halfway through the project, I was looking at the project critical path. The tool was cluttering the critical path with lots of unimportant activities. Other longer and more important activities were not on the path. Next time I run a project, I am going to move the more important activities onto the critical path, so I can place the proper amount of management focus on them."

I decided at this point to put on my coach's hat. The discussion on key learning from the project was a good one, but I did not want them to encounter other problems on their next project because of faulty understanding of the critical path.

LESSON 25

UNDERSTAND THE CRITICAL PATH ON YOUR PROJECT AND HOW THIS PATH DRIVES THE DEADLINE DATE

Before we discuss the critical path, let's first make sure we understand our definition of schedule float. *Float*, or *slack*, refers to a time lag that can occur between two activities without impacting the final deadline. For instance, let's say we have two activities—A and B. Activity B must start after activity A has finished. If activity B must start right away, there is zero slack. However, if activity B can start two days after activity A finishes without impacting the overall deadline date, then activity B has two days of slack. This does not mean activity B must wait two days. However, if necessary, activity B could wait up to two days without impacting the overall project deadline.

With that in mind, let's look at the critical path. "Critical path" is the name given to the sequence of activities that must be started and completed on time for the entire project to complete on time. There is no float, or slack, for any activity on the path. Every project has a critical path of activities, and the project end date is based on the length of time to complete the tasks on the critical path.

For example, imagine a project takes 300 days. The critical path might consist of a sequence of 40 activities that would also take 300 days to complete. If the first activity on the critical path is 1 day late, the project will take 301 days to complete, unless another activity on the critical path can be completed 1 day earlier.

It is vital the project manager understands the critical path and pays special attention to these activities, since any delay on the critical path will result in a delay in the entire project. At the same time, the project cannot be accelerated by speeding up activities off the critical path. If the project manager is not aware of the critical path and how it drives the project end date, it's likely that precious resources will be misapplied on the wrong activities.

Calculating critical path requires a forward pass and a backward pass through the schedule to determine which activities have float and which ones do not. The forward and backward passes are not difficult, but they can be very tedious. For that reason, the critical path is typically generated as a standard feature of your workplan scheduling software.

There are two common misconceptions about the critical path. The first is that all of the activities on the path are important, or "critical." The name "critical path" implies that the activities are, well, critical. However, this is not necessarily the case. While some activities on the path can be very important, it is also likely that many mundane and noncritical activities are there as well. Notice the definition of critical path talked about zero float. The definition did not say anything about how important or "critical" the activities were. In fact, the activities on the critical path are critical from a scheduling perspective, but they may or may not be of critical importance to the project.

The second misconception is the project manager can add "critical," or important, activities to the critical path. This is what I am hearing from Ashley at her end-of-project meeting. She would like to have all her "critical" (important) activities added to the critical path because she perceives she will spend more time focusing on the activities there. She is right about the additional scrutiny, but she has a basic misconception about how the critical path is calculated, and how the activities get there.

When I put on my coaching hat in this meeting, I explained the critical path to Ashley and the others. The critical path is what it is, and the project manager cannot add activities to it just because those activities are important. In fact, if new activities are forced onto the critical path, the result will be a delay on the project. For instance, if you arbitrarily forced a 10-day activity onto our 300-day project mentioned earlier, the result would be that the project takes 310 days to complete. That is not what you want.

I complemented Ashley on her desire to place more focus on certain activities, but asked her to determine the most important activities and place the appropriate level of focus on those—regardless of whether they were on the critical path or not.

26

Jerry Is Told to "Sharpen His Pencil" to Reduce an Estimate

Working with Jerry for the last six months has been a real treat for me. When Jerry first started his project to update the phone mail system, he was inexperienced and had no idea how to approach project management in an efficient and organized fashion. Now he was much more knowledgeable. He wasn't a seasoned pro by any means, but he had come a long way in a short time. I caught a bite after work with him a few weeks back to celebrate the completion of his project to upgrade the phone system and software. So far, there have been very few complaints and an abundance of compliments on a job well done.

In fact, Jerry did such a good job on the phone project he was given another big assignment: deploying an operating system upgrade on all Mega Manufacturing desktops. It was a large project and involved more team members and more responsibility, but Jerry's confidence was high and I could tell he felt capable of handling the job. His confidence was noteworthy, especially given where he was just a few months ago. It was also significant considering he and his wife would be moving into the Morettis' house in a few weeks. Clearly the organizational skills and confidence gained at work were carrying over into his personal life, because he showed no signs of stress or worry about the move.

Jerry came to see me at the end of June to discuss feedback he had received from his manager on the desktop upgrade project. Jerry's manager had just read his draft Project Definition. Apparently, he liked the overall definition and plan, but had a problem with the cost estimate.

"Are you ready for your big move, Jerry?" I asked as he entered the office.

"We sure are, Tom. Barbara already has a list of things she wants to change after we move in. We are both really excited."

"Are you planning any major changes?"

"Not at all. Barb wants to do some painting in certain rooms to better match our color schemes, and we are thinking about changing the tile in the master bathroom. Small things really."

"Sounds good. As always, let me know how I can help. So tell me, where are things with your project?"

"Well, I'm not sure what to do next," Jerry began. "I worked with a number of technical experts to prepare the effort and cost estimate for this project, but my manager said it is too high."

"Did your manager give you any insight as to why he thought the estimate was too high?" I asked.

"As best I can tell, the estimate is too high because it's more than the budget allocated for this work," Jerry explained. "He said if the numbers were closer to budget, he would just go ahead, but our estimate is 60 percent more than the initial budget allocation."

"Really?" I asked. "Well, the original budget was proposed last year during the business planning process. Those numbers are put forward at a pretty high level. It is not surprising your more detailed estimate is much higher. It's also probably much more accurate. Did your boss have any advice for you on how to reduce the number?"

"Not really," he replied. "He just said he wanted me to 'sharpen my pencil' some more and try to get the project estimate down substantially. This really stinks!"

"Hang in there," I said encouragingly. "You should not be forced into making an estimate you don't believe in. However, let's look at some options that might help you out."

LESSON 26

CHANGE THE UNDERLYING ASSUMPTIONS TO REVISE A WELL-PREPARED ESTIMATE

Jerry is not the first person to have an estimate questioned, and he will not be the last. This scenario happens all the time. Jerry's situation is a common one. The project to upgrade the desktop operating system was proposed and approved last year as a part of the business planning process. The company also allocated a preliminary budget to the work. However, most people don't have the time to perform a detailed effort and cost estimate for each project during the yearly planning process. Those budgets are estimated at a high level, and need to be validated once the actual project starts.

That's where we are now. Jerry was assigned to the project and is defining and planning the work at a lower level of detail. As a result, Jerry has created a much more realistic estimate of the costs involved, and his new figures are 60 percent higher than the original budget. The company expects the estimates to be off somewhat. In fact, Jerry's boss told him if his estimate was closer to the original budget, they could go back and ask for more money. However, his boss feels he will not be able to ask for a 60 percent increase. That type of increase will either not be funded at all, or the additional funding will probably require another approved project to be cancelled.

This puts Jerry in a tough position. The company wants to do the work—that's why it was approved for this year. However, now they may not be able to afford it. Jerry's boss wants the estimate reduced and has asked Jerry to "sharpen his pencil." On the surface, Jerry's manager is asking him to make the estimate more accurate. However, the clear implication is he wants the estimate reduced. His boss is assuming Jerry's estimate is sloppy or has some inherent padding that can be removed.

Jerry's first thought is that he needs to reduce the estimate arbitrarily, and then take the heat when the work comes in over budget. That is definitely not the path to take. Instead, he should look at two areas.

First, Jerry needs to verify his own estimate. If he used an estimating tool or a spreadsheet, he should double-check the formulas, check he is using the right resource rates, and make sure the nonlabor costs are reasonably accurate. Once he is convinced his math is accurate, Jerry should also see if there is at least one other estimating technique he can use for validation. It sounds like he relied on expert opinions to prepare the original estimate. He should also estimate the work at a low level against his work breakdown structure (or his project workplan if he is at that level). Since the work is fairly repetitive on thousands of workstations, he should also look for some estimating algorithm that could lead to a logical and reasonable number.

Second, Jerry should look at his estimating assumptions. All estimates are based on a set of explicit and implied assumptions. This is a time to look for creative ways to get the work done with less cost and effort, such as the following:

- *Look for less-costly alternatives:* This is a process of looking at all costs associated with the project to see if less-expensive alternatives exist that will accomplish the same thing. For instance, if you are counting on contract labor resources, you can see whether they could be replaced with employees. If you are proposing new software, see whether your company already has something that will work. Evaluate whether existing hardware can be utilized, rather than buying new machines. If you have training costs in your budget, see whether the training can be done in-house, rather than sending people to formal off-site classes. Remember, the purpose of this step is to see if there are alternatives that will allow you to reduce costs while still delivering all the required functionality.

- *Look for process improvements:* This step involves looking at how you propose to do the work to see if alternative approaches or techniques exist that will result in less effort and cost. For instance, if you have trips planned, determine whether some or all of the work can be accomplished with phone calls or teleconferences. See whether some manual processes can be automated. Perhaps a focused group meeting can be utilized to gather requirements instead off traditional one-on-one interview sessions. It may be possible to outsource some of the work at less cost than it would take to do it internally. Again, the purpose of this step is to deliver as planned, while requiring less effort.

- *Negotiate a reduction in scope:* The two preceding options allow you to deliver all the work requested, for less effort and cost than was originally proposed. This third option looks for activities or parts of the project that can be eliminated. Removing work should result in reduced effort and cost. Although all of the work on the project may have originally been seen as important, it usually turns out some components of the project are more important than others. In some instances, work can be deferred until a later date, perhaps when a new budget is available. This may result in a less-than-perfect solution, but one still acceptable to your sponsor. Jerry needs to go back and revisit the estimate with these points in mind. He may find there are ways to pare down the estimate, while delivering much of what the company needs. This exercise is not meant to force him into committing to a project budget he does not believe in. It is simply meant as an honest effort to reduce the estimated cost and effort.

Jerry owes his manager a complete account of how the estimate was prepared. If, at the end of this process, Jerry's estimate is still too high, he must ask for the assistance of his manager and other stakeholders to determine whether or how to proceed.

One option is to not do the project at all. If the cost of doing the project is more than the perceived benefit, it simply should not be done. Management stakeholders may have other options, including requesting the required incremental budget dollars if they are convinced additional money is justified.

After seeing Jerry's second estimate, including reasonable alternatives and options, his manager can determine how to proceed. If Jerry's estimate is still too high, his manager will need to take the new number forward for approval, or come up with some alternatives. If Jerry's estimate is closer to the original budget (even if the project scope has been reduced), his manager may be able to approve the work and let the project proceed. Either of these alternatives is better for Jerry and for the company than purposely underestimating the work, and then having to face the consequences later when the project goes over budget.

27 Jean Needs to Add a Personal Touch

Jean Combs was a tall woman with long, blonde hair. Her husband, Rick, was the head football coach at Northeast Illinois State, and a friend of my wife, Pam. Jean and Rick had a son, Dan, who was the same age as Tim, and the two boys were friends who got along very well when together. Jean was a quick learner when given new assignments, so when she called me to schedule an afternoon appointment, I knew something must have really stumped her on her project for the Finance Department.

"Come in, Jean! Good to see you. How are Rick and Dan?"

"They are both well, thanks for asking. Rick is busy interviewing candidates for defensive line coach at the university now that Jordan McKenzie has left for Purdue. He's a little worried since it is already July 1 and summer workouts are in progress. Of course, little Dan is still a bundle of energy, and has recently taken an interest in golf."

"That's funny! Tim has also shown some interest in golf. We'll have to get the two of them together sometime and play miniature golf."

"I am sure Dan would love that!"

"Tell you what, I'll give you a call over the weekend and we'll try to set something up. Now, what brings you to see me today?"

"Well, I could use some help on this project," she began. "It isn't in bad shape, but we missed a couple of milestone dates by less than a week. I think we are back on target now."

"That's good news," I said.

"Well, I wouldn't get too optimistic yet," she replied, trying to force a smile. "The overall workplan was very aggressive. What makes it frustrating is I received feedback from my sponsor and client manager recently saying we need to do a better job communicating what's going on. I've tried to communicate as much as possible, including sending out status reports. Not that anyone reads them."

"This project sounds very important to the Finance Department," I said with some surprise. "Why wouldn't they read the status reports?"

"It's just the way this project has gone," she replied frustratingly. "I don't think anyone reads the status reports. When we sent out e-mails to solicit requirements, we hardly received any replies. I send out e-mails whenever we have problems, but I do not get any help from the senior managers. We also publish risk plans, project news, and current status on a shared Web server, but very few clients read it. I think it's unfair of them to say now we are not communicating effectively."

It sounded like I had hit upon a pattern. "It certainly sounds like you have provided the clients with a lot of information," I noted. "However, when is the last time you met with them face to face?"

LESSON 27

DON'T SHORTCHANGE FACE-TO-FACE COMMUNICATION ON YOUR PROJECT

One of the key responsibilities of a project manager is to communicate proactively to clients, team members, and stakeholders. Some of this communication is routine and obvious, including status meetings and status reports. However, these communications are the minimum, and they do not satisfy the communication needs for most projects. If your project is large and impacts a substantial number of people, a Communication Plan should be created to try to meet the needs of all the stakeholders.

Since proactive communication is probably not her strong suit, Jean has found herself communicating in a manner that best suits her needs and not the needs of her clients and stakeholders. The approach is based purely on an electronic medium. Sure, it is easier to fire off e-mail messages. Yes, it might be quicker to place documentation on a shared Web server for stakeholders to read. The truth is, however, that this form of communication is only easier and quicker for Jean and it does not address the needs of her business clients at all.

To be fair, there is nothing wrong with Jean's communication. There is a place for e-mail messages, status reports, and Web sites. They are probably vital pieces in an overall Communication Plan. However, they should not be used as a way to avoid having to meet with your sponsor and client managers. There is no substitute for face-to-face meetings and personal communications.

Jean is facing a common IT problem. She is providing information, but it is not always delivered as effectively as it should be. She is comfortable working with her team members and the lower-level client users, but she is not as comfortable talking with the more senior client stakeholders.

Jean needs to understand that senior managers can receive hundreds of messages per day. They also have many initiatives going on at the same time. Your project is important to them, but they have many other competing priorities as well. It is not reasonable to assume they will always be able to sift through hundreds of e-mails to find the key bits of information relevant to the project.

This is not meant to be an excuse for them. The senior management stakeholders should have an interest in your project and should invest the time to make sure it has everything it needs to be successful. However, the project manager needs to make it easy for them. It is much more likely they will remember the things they hear about at meetings and from colleagues, even if the information is not entirely accurate.

It certainly looks like Jean is communicating. However, she has not found the right forum and format to provide her clients with the information they want to know. That is why, in spite of the communication Jean has done, the clients are still telling her she needs to communicate more. Actually, it appears they are saying they would like Jean to communicate more effectively with them.

My advice to Jean is to follow up with the sponsor and client manager to get their feedback on additional ways the project team can communicate with them. For instance, Jean may need to set up periodic briefings for the sponsor and other senior stakeholders. The e-mails and status reports will then be much more effective as a means of filling in the blanks between personal meetings. This will provide more effective, accurate, and reliable information for them and make them more comfortable communicating directly with her if they have further questions. Jean can also take advantage of the meetings to ask for things important to her, like feedback on problems.

28 Erika's Quality Plan Needs More Quality

I had been trying to cut back on my coffee intake lately. Not that I was "Mr. Healthy," but I guess every little bit helped. Who needed all that caffeine anyway? Part of the plan was to avoid drinking coffee at home in the morning, and instead drink water or juice. I hadn't been drinking my first cup of coffee until after I got to work and checked my e-mail. This morning I was returning from the break room with my first cup when I ran into Erika Thompson.

Erika was wearing a black skirt with a red blouse, and she had on flag-shaped earrings (it was July 3). Her husband, Martin, who was in the Army, was stationed overseas on an eight-month tour of duty. The Fourth of July was very meaningful to her, because her father was killed in combat during the Vietnam War. She visited Washington, D.C., last year with her husband, and I remembered her saying it was a moving experience, especially visiting the Vietnam Memorial.

"I see you are ready for Independence Day," I said as she waved her hand at me.

"You bet I am, although it will be tough with Martin away from home."

"When does his tour of duty end, Erika? Seems like he has been gone for quite some time."

"He left right after Christmas last year, so he'll be back in a few months. I can hardly wait!"

"I bet. Your frantic wave makes me think you have something on your mind besides fireworks though."

"You're right," she said, taking a deep breath. "I have heard you talk in the past about the need for building quality into your solution. I have a team building a new employee self-service module onto our benefits system. I wanted to let you know that we have just built a Quality Plan. We wanted to do something because Human Resources has a lot of sensitive information, and we need to make sure the information is accurate and secure."

I was pleased. "Great," I said. "I think you will find building quality into your process will save you effort and cost over the entire project. Tell me about your plan."

"We have done a number of things," she explained. "First, we have a 'Quality Day' scheduled every two weeks. That's the time we check the results of everyone's work to date. Second, we have designated a person to check the entire self-service application when it is completed to find any errors we may have missed. Third, we have asked one of our clients to be responsible for the overall quality of the solution. With these kinds of checks in place, we should end up with a good product."

I thought for a minute. On the surface, all of this sounded good, but something wasn't quite right. "Erika," I asked, "what are your developers doing in between the 'Quality Days?'"

"They are working hard to build this module," she explained. "In fact, they think they can get more work done since they know reviews will be done every other week, and that someone will double-check the application at the end of the project."

This was starting to confirm my suspicions. "Let's talk a little further about your plan. Building quality into your solution needs to be an integral part of your development process. It appears you have a series of quality events, but you want to make sure people are taking personal responsibility for quality as well."

LESSON 28

MAKE SURE QUALITY IS A MINDSET AND AN ONGOING PROCESS ON YOUR PROJECT

A quality product meets the agreed upon expectations of the client. Repeatedly capturing errors and fixing them can accomplish a high quality of delivery, but it is a very inefficient process. The best approach is to build a quality product the first time. In general, your team cannot build a quality product the first time without quality work processes.

Building a quality product also requires the team to have a quality mindset. They need to be personally concerned about quality, and they need to take personal responsibility for building a quality product. The team needs to be constantly looking for ways to do things right the first time, and looking for ways to capture any defects as early as possible after they have been introduced.

It appears Erika's team has great intentions. In fact, her approach may be better than doing nothing at all, since it does at least heighten everyone's awareness of the need for quality. However, she appears to have made three mistakes that may negate her team's good intentions.

First, although there is not a problem with focusing on quality on a scheduled basis, she needs to ensure her team does not see quality as a series of events. Her team members must see quality as a daily aspect of their job. Let's look at her biweekly "Quality Day." On the surface, there is nothing wrong with it. However, consider Erika's comment about the team getting more work done since they can catch errors on "Quality Day." Erika needs to be careful her team members are not producing lower-quality work, since they see "Quality Day" as a time to catch all the errors. If that is the case (and it sounds like it is), then her team members are not taking personal responsibility for getting their work done right the first time. They may also be viewing quality as a biweekly event, instead of a continuous process.

Second, they have designated a person to check all work at the end of the project. Again, this may be fine as long as it is a final inspection in an ongoing quality process. But Erika needs to be sure team members are not producing work of poor quality based on the assumption that someone else is responsible for catching errors later on. Catching errors at the end of the project is better than not catching them at all, but generally this is the worst time to catch them. Errors caught at the end of the project are the most costly and time consuming to correct. Catching errors early is a much better approach.

Third, designating a client to be in charge of overall quality appears to shift the responsibility as well. There is nothing wrong with the client being involved. However, in a quality environment, the project team needs to be responsible for quality. In fact, each person must be responsible for his or her work. The client may be asked to help verify the final product meets her expectations, but she should not be responsible for the work others are producing.

Erika's quality plan should be revised in these areas. First, she can schedule walkthroughs and testing inspections throughout the development process—not just at arbitrary biweekly "Quality Days." Her team should understand that each of them is responsible for the work they produce. Others are not responsible for catching their errors. Lastly, although the client can take ownership of the testing process and can verify the final solution meets her expectations, the overall responsibility for quality must remain with the team building the solution. These changes will ensure the team has a quality mindset and takes responsibility for the application they are building.

29 Sean Is Losing the Deadline Battle—a Little at a Time

Sean Robinson had been in the IT Application Support organization for almost 15 years, and was one of the best. He knew our marketing applications inside and out, and always knew where to find the answers if they weren't already in his head. Like many support specialists, however, Sean was not the strongest project manager. Perhaps that's the nature of good support people. They are used to jumping in and fixing problems quickly. A long activity for him might have been 20 hours. Maybe that was why it was tough for him to develop the patience and structured thinking required to plan and manage larger projects.

In spite of these shortcomings, Sean was often asked to manage projects to enhance current marketing applications, and he had enough knowledge and experience to deliver small enhancement projects reasonably close to expectations. Sean was also open and willing to learn structured project management techniques—at least up to a point. I talked to Sean recently about his current project. He was a little apprehensive.

Sean said the purpose of his project was to track the response rates of direct mail campaigns. The project was projected to last for four months, and had started last month on June 15. Unfortunately, the project was already at risk of exceeding its budget and deadline. I asked a standard series of questions about how he was managing the project, to see if I could identify some root causes for why the project was in trouble. I asked about the workplan, deliverables, risks, staffing, issues, etc. When we got to scope change management, Sean was a little defensive.

"You know, I am more than willing to use formal project management techniques when they make sense," Sean said, running his hand through his thick blonde hair. "But you know Marketing. They always want changes after agreeing to the initial scope. I would like to use good scope change management, but the changes are always small. You know, five hours here,

three hours there. Pretty soon you are talking about some real hours. I think that's why we are in trouble."

"Let's talk about your scope change procedures," I said. "Can you tell me how you are managing these small changes?"

"Our scope management process normally includes gaining sponsor approval for changes," Sean said. "But am I the only person who has a busy sponsor? I can't take every two-hour scope change request to him. He would throw me out of his office. So, we are trying to be client focused and fit as many of these small changes in as possible. What other options do I have?"

"Obviously, you don't want to bother your sponsor for every small scope change request," I said. "However, there is another option. Let's talk about this further."

LESSON 29

BATCH SMALL SCOPE CHANGE REQUESTS TOGETHER FOR SPONSOR APPROVAL

I can sympathize with Sean. He thinks he has done a good job by establishing scope, and he is prepared to handle scope changes by taking the change requests to the sponsor, along with the project impact assessment. However, he also knows the sponsor is busy and does not want to be bothered with "minor" scope changes. Sean is probably right. Most likely, the sponsor does not want to be bothered with every two- and four-hour scope change request. There are a couple alternatives, however.

First, it may be perfectly acceptable for the project manager and the main client manager to have some discretionary power to approve small scope changes, as long as the changes do not impact the team's ability to deliver the project on time and within budget. The sponsor will need to agree to this delegation of authority and then it can be added to the scope change process. If small change requests are submitted, they must still be documented, including estimating the project impact and the business value. This process does not need to be elaborate. Each request could simply take up one line of your Scope Change Log.

Before you get too excited, however, note the key caveat mentioned earlier. This discretionary authority can be used only if there is no impact on the project timeline and budget. This will not help Sean, since he stated he is already at risk of going over schedule and budget.

In Sean's case, he should utilize a second management technique for small changes—batching small scope changes together. This still means keeping track of the small scope changes, their business value, and their impact on the project. When they hit a certain threshold, you take all of them to the sponsor for approval. The threshold could be reached when the impact of the scope changes exceeds a target—for instance, 100 hours. The threshold could also be in terms of the number of small requests received—for instance, ten small requests.

The result is that, instead of visiting the sponsor ten times for ten small scope changes, you batch them all together and see the sponsor once only for each batch of changes. At that meeting, you, the client manager, and the sponsor discuss all the proposed changes and get sponsor feedback on whether they should be done. The benefit of having the sponsor approve the changes is he or she can also approve the incremental budget and time needed to get the work done.

Keep in mind, however, that just as this idea of batching requests may be new to the project manager, it may also be new to the sponsor. Therefore, be sure to explain to the sponsor the efficiency associated with handling small scope changes this way. In fact, if you utilize this technique, you may find the sponsor has little patience and sympathy for small scope change requests that add only small incremental business value. As was mentioned in lesson 11, sponsors typically do not want to be distracted from the main business objectives. If the final solution meets 80 percent of their needs, they are typically happy. They normally don't care to add too many small requests that may only result in the solution meeting 82 percent of their needs. Although Sean might hesitate to say "no" to scope change requests, the sponsor typically does not have that problem. Usually they are more than happy to say "no."

Sean's last comment on being client focused is telling. His team is trying to be client focused by agreeing to include as many small changes as possible. However, is this really being client focused? If the project goes over budget and over its deadline, will the sponsor talk about how client focused Sean is? Probably not. Instead, the sponsor will probably talk about how the team missed its commitments.

The best thing Sean can do to be client focused is to meet his commitments on project budget and deadline. His major client is the sponsor. With his project now at risk, he should ensure no scope changes are agreed to without sponsor approval, and a corresponding increase in budget and schedule.

30 Jerry Jumps into the Workplan Too Quickly

STEP 1 DEFINE THE WORK

Pam and I took Tim to the department store during the last weekend in July to shop for back-to-school items. Tim was starting kindergarten in the fall, and we wanted to spark some excitement in him by buying a few supplies. The school had sent us a welcome pack over the summer, including a sheet of required tools. It was the usual fare of pencils, pens, glue, crayons, scissors, etc. The first thing we bought was a black-and-red backpack with golf balls on it. Tim and I had been practicing golf quite a bit over the summer, and I promised to take him to a real course next year.

Leaving the department store, we drove to the Morettis' old house to have dinner with Jerry and Barbara. They had invited us over to see the new place, and I was excited to see what they had done with it. As we pulled into the driveway, I could already see one big change. Jerry had pulled the bushes out from around the house and replaced them with flower gardens. There was also a nice bed of flowers planted around the mailbox in the front of the yard.

On the inside, things were mostly the same, but with all new furniture. Jerry said they were still going to paint, but thought they would plant the flowerbeds first while it was still warm outside. "Good project management decision," I said jokingly. Jerry led me down to the basement, and I was surprised to see the shelves covered in beer steins, just as they were when Wayne lived there.

"I thought that might surprise you," Jerry said as I looked around. "A nice gift from Wayne. He left me all his beer steins. He said he didn't have much use for them in Arizona, and he knew how much I admired them when I saw them for the first time. I told Wayne I would continue to display them and that he should let me know if he ever decided he wanted them back."

Jerry showed me some of his favorite steins and then grabbed a couple beers out of the refrigerator in the bar. Handing one to me, he asked if I would mind talking shop for a few minutes. He was still in the early stages of his new project to deploy an operating system upgrade on all of our desktops, and he said his head was still swimming with too much information.

"As you can imagine, the technical considerations for this project are not difficult," Jerry began carefully. "Upgrading a workstation is easy. However, when you have thousands of workstations, the complexity of completing the entire project starts to get overwhelming. The timing and scheduling are very complicated. I have started to think through a number of scenarios, and the permutations seem endless. There are many, many ways we could proceed."

"I can imagine the difficulty," I empathized. "But, if you have a number of ways to get the work done, does it really matter which one you choose?"

"I think you're right," Jerry agreed. "But it's been hard for me to lay out any detailed plan from beginning to end. I get halfway through one plan, and then I start to see multiple options. As I work through the options, the details get more complicated. Then I start to lose track of the overall pros and cons of the scenario I am following. Even worse, I am afraid when I do finalize a plan, not everyone is going to like it."

"Jerry, when you are defining a project, one of the areas you look at is the overall approach," I said. "Have you completed that work yet?"

"Actually, that's what I am trying to do now," he replied. "I will be able to define the approach once I think through the details and the implications."

"In some projects that might work," I said. "But a complex project workplan should be built from the top down. If you define and gain agreement on the overall approach first, you can build the detailed workplan much more easily."

LESSON 30

DEFINE THE OVERALL PROJECT APPROACH BEFORE BUILDING THE DETAILED WORKPLAN

Part of the definition process for a large project should be defining and communicating the overall project approach. Put simply, the project approach contains three elements:

- A high-level description of the phases (the high-level related sections of work) needed to complete the project.

- An understanding of the relationship between the phases. For instance, you can define the major deliverables completed in each phase and whether they are utilized in subsequent phases. You can also note whether a phase has unique resource needs not required on the rest of the project.

- An explanation of any special or unusual techniques that may be required. For instance, if you are going to gather business requirements by sequestering all the stakeholders in an off-site meeting for a week, you should note this in the approach.

The purpose of defining an approach is to put the workplan into words that managers and stakeholders can understand and use as the basis for their review of how the project will progress. Your sponsor, for instance, is not going to want to pore over the details of a long project workplan. Even if he or she did, it would be hard to look at the detailed workplan and get a sense for how the project will progress. However, if the sponsor reads the project approach, he or she can get the overall vision.

The project approach is not needed for all projects. It is easier to envision what needs to happen in smaller projects, and documenting an overall approach would not add much value. However, documenting the overall approach is important for large and complex projects.

If the project is complicated or if there are many options, the approach should be defined and agreed to first, before the workplan is built. This has two advantages. First, it allows the project manager to lay out a plan for successfully completing the work at a high level, instead of trying to put all of the details into a workplan all at once. Second, and perhaps more important, it allows the project manager to gain a consensus on the best way to execute the project at a high level.

Jerry's project provides a great example of the importance of defining an approach first. His project is not complex from a technical standpoint, but it is very complex from an implementation perspective. Think about how he could deploy the desktop upgrade. He could upgrade workstations in alphabetical order of the user's last name. He could (and perhaps should) upgrade all the workstations in a department all at one time. But what is the order? For instance, should he upgrade the IT department first? Perhaps the company executives should go first, or perhaps they should go last. Political implications might affect the scheduling as well. As Jerry noted, he might come up with an acceptable plan, but it may not be accepted for political reasons or other unknown reasons.

Jerry's tendency to want to execute before planning has resulted in trying to lay out the detailed activity in a workplan rather than defining a high-level project approach first. Instead, he should define an overall approach and then start circulating it for feedback and input. His sponsor and other management stakeholders can come to an agreement with Jerry on the overall deployment approach. At that point, Jerry won't have many permutations for executing the project. He will only have one. He can then break down the agreed approach into lower-level activities for the workplan. If he finds places in the workplan where there are multiple options to proceed, he can make appropriate decisions based on the framework of the overall approach. In general, the high-level definition of the project approach will save time and provide focus when he builds the more detailed workplan.

31

Danielle Is Sensing Risky Business

Tuesday of the last week of July was hot and muggy in Dickens. The weatherman predicted rain for the weekend, but next week, he said, would bring high humidity and temperatures in the 90s. Pam was attending a sports conference in Chicago, and Tim and I had plans for a "guy's weekend" of eating pizza and watching the Cubs play a series at Cincinnati on TV. Tim liked watching the Cubs play, although he still had a hard time sitting through nine innings of baseball. Usually, by about the fourth inning, I would have to pull out a deck of cards or a board game to play.

I had just gotten off the phone with Pam when Danielle Bartlett came by for her 11 a.m. meeting. When I last saw her, she was dressed from head to toe in black for Valentine's Day. This time she wore a colorful skirt and blouse and appeared to be much happier. I asked her why she was so happy.

"Well, believe it or not, I met a guy on Valentine's Day, and we've been dating for the last five months," she said as she walked into my office. "I met him buying beer at the grocery store. Turns out we were both alone on the dreaded day, so we got to talking and the rest is history."

"Wow, that's exciting," I replied. "I am glad to see you so happy. Also, I believe more congratulations are in order. I heard your project to implement a construction cost-estimating package was completed without a hitch."

"Thanks," Danielle smiled back. "However, I don't know if that was a good move or not. My boss thanked me by asking me to manage another project for the Facilities Department. Oh well, I guess that's why they pay me the big bucks!"

"Well, 'Ms. Big Bucks,' what have they got you doing now?"

"The Facilities Department works with a number of vendors and subcontractors. They think they can coordinate their work more effectively if they have a small intranet portal available that all of the vendors can link into. Then everyone can get common information and coordinate schedules more effectively."

"Great news!" I said in a purposely half-sarcastic tone.

"Hardly," she said, taking a seat in the chair in front of my desk. "I've been talking with the business clients and with my team members," she began. "They keep telling me this is a low-risk project and I should not be worried. But I am very uncomfortable right now."

"Why are they saying this is a low-risk project?" I asked.

"The people from Facilities know their business very well," she replied, fanning herself with a file folder. "They think they can create the content for this Web site portal with a minimum of effort from our IT team. We just need to set up the secure environment to begin with. In the short-term, however, many of the clients are starting to work on a major office renovation. They just use spreadsheets and e-mail today to coordinate work with the vendors and say anything would be better. The IT project team just wants to get going. They think they can overcome any problems that might pop up."

"That's the kind of approach that can get you into trouble," I said. "Sure, problems can be fixed, but at what cost to budget, schedule, and quality? What other things are making you uncomfortable?"

"I only have about nine months' experience with Web development work, and the two people on my team have less than me," Danielle answered. "This is also my first opportunity to manage a substantial Web project that requires third-party access. When I did background checking, I read about other companies having problems with this particular release. And besides that . . ."

"Whoa!" I interrupted. "Hold on a minute. I have picked out three or four risks in the last minute alone. I think you are right to be concerned about the overall project risk. It seems you are just having a hard time isolating the risks and articulating them. Let me find a risk assessment form for you to look at. It contains characteristics of projects that bring inherent risks with them. Once you have identified all your high risks, you can put risk plans in place to respond to them."

LESSON 31

LOOK FOR RISKS INHERENT TO YOUR PROJECT BEFORE YOU BEGIN

Sometimes it is easy to look at a project and see risks. For instance, you may have a fixed deadline that will be hard to achieve, or you may have a need for specialists you know will be hard to find. Both of these situations are better than the times you think a project will be easy because you fail to identify hidden risks.

The place to start looking for potential project risks is in the project characteristics. Some project characteristics, by their very nature, imply higher risk. An example of inherent risk is project size. A project requiring 500 effort hours has less inherent risk than one requiring 5,000 effort hours, or one requiring 50,000 hours. If you knew nothing else at all about the project, you could say the larger project of 50,000 hours is riskier than the project of 500 hours. More effort hours means more people to manage, more budget to control, and more chances for staff turnover. In general, there is more of a chance for people-related problems. Increased complexity in any form typically means increased inherent risk.

Let's look at Danielle's project. She is uneasy about the risk associated with the project. Her client is telling her it's no big deal, but she knows better. Based on our discussion, we identified the following potential risks:

- She and her team are fairly new to the intranet/Web technical world and do not have a deep understanding of how it all works. This makes for more risk than if they had experienced people on the team. This is an example of an inherent risk, since any project is riskier if the team is inexperienced.

- This is Danielle's first opportunity to manage a substantial project that requires interaction with vendors. Her lack of experience could be a big risk. This is also an example of an inherent risk, since any major project with a less-experienced project manager will be riskier than one with an experienced project manager.

- It appears the client may not have the time to focus on this project because of another large initiative. There is an inherent risk whenever there is a question about the commitment of your client.

Inherent risks are based on the general characteristics of a project rather than the specific circumstances of your project. Since they are general in nature, they can be identified and placed in a checklist for all project managers to review. This should be the starting point for the risk identification process. If you identify an inherent risk, determine whether it is a high risk for your project or something lower. If you find high risks (or perhaps medium risks) inherent, it does not mean that the project should not go forward. It simply means the project manager should focus risk plans in those areas of identified risk in order to minimize the potential for problems during the project.

32 | Mike Receives a Change Request He Needs to "Scope" Out

STEP 5 MANAGE SCOPE

Mike Miller and I had not worked together for several months, but we had played basketball last weekend at a park near my house, and he had mentioned some problems he was having with a new project to install document management software at our worldwide regional headquarters. In fact, his team had fallen behind on the project. Mike was very laid-back, and did not appear to be too worried about the delays, but I asked him to drop by my office on Tuesday to discuss things.

"Come on in Mike. Thanks for the game last weekend!"

"Sure thing, Coach. Hope you weren't too sore that night!" Mike was a bit of a bruiser, especially on the boards. Every time he missed a shot, he banged into me as I tried to get the rebound. It was a friendly game, but with a lot of physical contact. I had been a bit sore after our game, but I did not want Mike to know about it.

"I felt great. There's nothing like a little basketball in August to get you sweating. I haven't played that hard since my college days!" I replied. "After the game you mentioned you were falling behind on your project. What's the story there?"

"Actually, we aren't too bad right now. But we have just received a change request that may cause us some trouble. You know we recently installed document management software for the Legal Department here in the headquarters. Now we have a new project to install a similar system for our other Legal Departments in Tokyo and London. However, our London client had some off-the-wall ideas that will require making substantial customizations to the standard package because of some differences in how the London office operates."

"A substantial change could require replanning the entire project," I replied. "I hope you invoked your scope change procedures. This is clearly something not envisioned when your project started."

"Yes, it's definitely a scope change," Mike agreed. "Unfortunately, I can already see where this is heading. We can't make a change of this magnitude and still hit our end-of-year deadlines for completing both offices. So, we will spend two weeks looking at the impact to the project and preparing a cost estimate. I'm certain the change request will not be approved, but we will still be held accountable for hitting our original delivery date."

"Do your scope change procedures say anything about how much time you will spend on investigations?" I asked.

"No," Mike said. "They only say we will investigate the request to determine the impact to the project in terms of effort, cost, and duration. The sponsor will then decide if we proceed or not."

"That sounds like a good beginning, but you've missed something," I concluded. "There is another scope change request that needs to be taken to your sponsor."

Mike looked puzzled. "What other scope change?" he asked.

"This may be hard to follow at first," I said slowly. "But the analysis required for the scope change is itself a scope change. It is a substantial piece of work you did not count on, and it will impact your effort and schedule. You need to check with the sponsor before even undertaking the investigation."

LESSON 32

GET SPONSOR APPROVAL BEFORE INVESTIGATING LARGE SCOPE CHANGE REQUESTS

When you create your initial project estimates, you need to include time and effort hours for project management activities. On most projects, the recognized standard is to add 15 percent. This covers the time it takes to manage the workplan, to assign work, to communicate effectively, and to manage risks, etc. The time it takes to manage the scope change process is included in this percentage as well. For instance, if you estimate a project to take 1,000 effort hours, the time allocated for project management would be around 150 hours, making the final estimate 1,150 effort hours.

The 15 percent rule assumes you have typical project management activities. It is possible you could go over that amount, depending on the type of manager you are. Some project management activities can make you go higher as well. For instance, if your project plan is complex, or if you have to replan the work based on resource changes, then you could exceed that amount.

Scope change requests would not normally require you to exceed your project management estimates. Typically, you just need to guide the requests through a process. If the scope changes are approved, you should receive the appropriate budget and schedule adjustments.

Some scope change requests, however, require a substantial amount of time to investigate and to estimate. These relatively large scope change requests are not taken into account in the 15 percent project management overhead. For instance, let's look again at the earlier example of a project that requires 1,000 effort hours and 150 hours for project management. If you receive a major scope change request that will take 80 hours to investigate, you are obviously going to have trouble fitting it within your project management time.

The project manager needs to recognize the potential impact on a project when a request comes in requiring scope change management. The project manager must also recognize the impact that the investigation associated with a scope change request may have on the project. In these instances, the key is to engage the sponsor very early on in the scope change life cycle. The sponsor needs to understand the nature of the request and then decide if the value of the investigation is worth the impact to the project.

Mike is in that position today. His project management budget was not built to take into account a major scope change investigation like this. Therefore, the investigation itself is out of scope. Rather than charge ahead with the investigation, Mike should take this request to the sponsor immediately. In essence, he should follow his normal scope change management process. Unless the business value is high enough to approve the schedule disruption, the sponsor will probably reject the request, and leave the original scope intact. If Mike is correct in his view that his sponsor would probably not approve the software customizations, it is likely he will not approve the scope change investigation either. However, if the sponsor does approve the investigation, and its impact on the project, then the budget and schedule can be adjusted accordingly to absorb this additional work.

33 Chucky May Be Crazy About Collecting Metrics

Charles Riley was an intense man with a great sense of humor, who was known to work very long hours. His colleagues nicknamed him "Chucky," after the crazy doll portrayed in the movie Child's Play, because, they said, of his crazy intensity and laser beam focus. I had never met him before, but was told by a colleague that his reputation for being intense was justified. My colleague also said he was a very funny man who appreciated a good joke and loved telling one. I was looking forward to our meeting.

He arrived right on time for our 2 p.m. meeting and got right to the point. He explained his team was nearing the midpoint on his project to develop a new employee datamart for the Payroll Department. Part of the business justification for this project was the productivity increase that would result from the payroll managers being able to write their own ad-hoc requests for information. The sponsor wanted Charles to try to measure this benefit. This would require estimating the time it took to gather information today using their manual spreadsheets. This would give them baseline information to see whether the new datamart software allowed them to do the same functions more efficiently.

Charles began with his dilemma. "We built time into our workplan to collect these productivity metrics, but we only allocated time for members of the project team. We didn't take into account the time needed from the payroll managers. These managers are complaining about having to measure and track this information. They are busy, and don't have the time to spare to collect a lot of extra information."

"What information are you trying to collect?" I asked.

"We gave them a template to track how long it currently takes to find the information that they need, so that we can compare it with the length of time it will take when we install the new software. The problem is the users get many requests each week, and it takes extra diligence to stop and document what they are doing."

"Well, maybe they have a point. Everything we do on a project, including the collection of metrics, needs to make sense from a cost/benefit perspective," I said. "How much time does it take to fill out the template?"

"Some of the people are saying it takes a lot of time. But we're not really sure right now," he replied.

"You need to start by understanding the time and cost of collecting the metrics. Sometimes people don't like to do new things based on emotion and a resistance to change. However, sometimes the pushback is based on facts. It may, in fact, be disruptive to their daily routine. Your team will need to dig deeper to understand the effort associated with the collection of this metric, and work with your sponsor to make sure the value received is worth this effort. I'm not suggesting it is too much time. I am only saying you should estimate the impact of collecting the metrics before you start."

LESSON 33

MAKE SURE THE COST OF COLLECTING METRICS DOES NOT EXCEED THEIR VALUE

Collecting meaningful data to help make business decisions is a good thing. In fact, most organizations would be better off if they had more information about how they were doing their jobs. However, the value to the business that you can attain by collecting this information has to be analyzed in the light of the costs of collecting this information. A problem occurs when the time and cost to collect the data is more than the value of the resulting information.

The best metrics are those easily generated by a computer. They are automatically collected at a certain time, and reports can be generated to show information in many ways. Financial information is usually presented in this way. Most companies have automated general ledgers, billing, accounts receivable, and other accounting software. If this is the case with your company, you'll find it relatively easy to gather information on how you are doing against your budget.

Project teams, however, don't usually have the luxury of automated metrics collection. Projects are not usually long or large enough to create complicated and automated applications to collect metrics. In other instances, there is not a good way to automate the collection process. Therefore, much of what gets collected is done manually.

For metrics requiring manual collection efforts (from users or project team members), there are three questions to ask:

- How much effort and cost does it take to gather the information?
- Are there less expensive, alternative metrics that will approximate the same result?
- Is the value of the knowledge gained worth the effort and cost?

As usual, the definition of value is a matter of opinion of the person paying for the information—usually the sponsor.

Charles needs to ask these questions today. His sponsor would like to get some hard numbers on the productivity gains associated with their new application. Charles and his team have come up with a way to determine this value by comparing the time it takes using the manual processes today with the time that it will take to complete the same function with the datamart solution in place.

Charles has a good solution, but it may come at too high a price. He and his team need to do some analysis into the time and cost associated with having the users complete the reporting templates. If the time is very short, he can proceed to the third question and ask the sponsor if the cost of collection is worth the benefit.

On the other hand, Charles is already getting feedback from the client that the time taken to collect the information is high. This is not definitive since the sponsor is the one who makes the final decision—not the payroll managers. However, it would be to Charles's benefit to look for some alternatives. For instance, if the payroll managers collect the information for two days per week, can the total time estimate be extrapolated from there? Perhaps Charles can ask each person to estimate the amount of time he or she spends performing the activity at the end of each day. There would be less accuracy, but the effort and, therefore, the cost of collection would be reduced considerably as well.

Once Charles has more information on the cost of collecting the metrics, as well as some alternatives, he should ask the sponsor for feedback on how to proceed. It may be the sponsor is willing to have people collect very accurate data because of the resulting business value, or the sponsor may decide having less accuracy, but substantially reduced collection costs, is the way to go. In either case, Charles will find it easier to collect the metrics, since it is now the sponsor who has decided what metrics to capture.

34 | Alex Has 200 Projects to Estimate!

STEP 2 BUILD THE WORKPLAN

Alex Jordan was a divorced 45-year old father of two teenage boys. I had had limited interaction with him on the job, but when we did talk I found him to be shy and nervous. From everything I had heard, he was more comfortable behind a computer screen than he was in front of people. Still, though, he seemed like a nice enough guy, and no one had ever said anything bad about the quality of his work. He knocked on my door around 1:30 p.m. for our meeting to discuss his project.

Alex was responsible for a project to upgrade an old version of our standard database management software. First, he needed to put together an estimate of the effort required to complete the project.

"I need to put together a high-level estimate for this project, and I am having a hard time figuring out where to begin. We have more than 200 databases in our environment, and they each bring their own complexities. I don't have time to do 200 individual estimates."

I first asked about estimating by analogy. "Have you discussed the project with the people who were responsible for installing the previous release? If you knew how much effort they had used, you might be able to estimate the effort for this one."

"I wish that were the case," Alex sighed. "However, the vendor is already telling us this new release will require a substantially larger amount of effort compared to that required for the previous release. I will be talking with the people who did the last upgrade, but it doesn't appear their experience can be leveraged for this project."

Next, I thought about estimating based on expert opinion. "Okay, is it possible to find someone else who has gone through this before? Perhaps someone at the database vendor or one of the research analysts could provide some insight."

"I'm afraid not," Alex sighed again. "We are one of the first companies to install the new release. The vendor is willing to help, since we will be one of their beta sites, but they don't want to put an estimate on the table because they don't know what our learning curve will be."

"Okay then, let's try a modeling approach, since much of the work will be similar once we understand exactly what is required," I explained. "We can do a paper migration for a complex, medium, and simple database and then apply some fairly easy math to estimate the total project effort."

LESSON 34

USE ONE OR MORE FORMAL TECHNIQUES TO ESTIMATE PROJECT WORK EFFORT

Many people have an intuitive sense for the duration and effort associated with certain types of work. However, when the work gets outside their comfort zone, they do not know how to put a logical estimate together.

Fortunately there are a number of formal techniques to estimate the work. It is hard to say whether one approach is always better than another. It depends on the project and the information available. There are some very complex and mathematically driven estimating techniques, but there are a number of simpler ones as well. The following techniques can be used at a project level or activity level, or for any work in between:

- *Previous history:* This is the best way to estimate work. If your organization keeps track of actual effort hours from previous projects, you may have information to help you estimate new work. Unfortunately, Mega Manufacturing, like most companies, does not save prior project metrics. So, Alex will not be able to use this specific technique.

- *Analogy:* Even if you do not keep actual effort hours from previous projects, you may still be able to leverage previous work. Analogy means you look for similar projects, even if you do not capture all of the relevant details associated with the previous approach. This may just mean sending an e-mail to various department managers describing your project and asking if they know of any similar projects. If you find one, you can talk to the project manager to see how many effort hours his or her project took, and use the information as input for your estimate. Alex initially tried this approach by talking to people who worked on the last database upgrade, but it appears their experience will not be applicable on this project.

- *Ratio:* Ratio is similar to analogy except you have some basis for comparing work with similar characteristics, but on a larger or smaller scale. For instance, you may find the effort required to complete a software installation at the Miami office was 500 hours. If there are twice as many people in the Chicago office, you may be able to deduce that the Chicago installation will take 1,000 hours. Actually, Alex can take advantage of this technique. He can gather information on the time it took the prior team to complete the upgrade and use that as a floor for his estimate. He would not expect his estimate to come at a lower level than this prior, less complex, upgrade.

- *Expert opinion:* In many cases you may need to go to an internal or external expert to get help estimating the work. Although this may be your first time estimating a certain piece of work, perhaps someone else has done it many times. Alex has tried this technique as well. He asked the vendor for help estimating the time to upgrade databases, because he was hoping they might have experts. The vendor declined to provide an estimate, since they did not have much experience with this release of their software. In fact, they would like Mega Manufacturing to be a beta site so they can gain experience from our project as well.

- *Work breakdown structure (WBS):* The WBS approach involves breaking work down into smaller and smaller pieces. This technique can be used to build a workplan, and can also be used to estimate work more easily. You may look at a large piece of work and have difficulty estimating the effort required. However, as the work is broken into smaller pieces, the individual components will be easier to estimate. When you have estimated all the pieces, add them together for the overall effort. If you have the time to create a good WBS, you will usually end up with a good estimate. In this case, the WBS approach is probably not the best one for Alex. The WBS will end up breaking down the work into the 200 or so database conversions, which is not much more information than he has today.

- *Modeling:* In this technique, you look for a pattern in the work, so an algorithm can be used to drive the overall estimate. For instance, if you know you can build one mile of flat, one-lane highway for $1 million, you should be able to easily calculate an estimate for ten miles of flat, four-lane highway ($40 million).

I think Alex can use a modeling approach for this estimate. He has 200 instances of database upgrades to perform. Although each of these instances is unique, there will obviously be many similarities as well. Alex needs to identify a number of unique cases he can use to categorize all 200 database conversions.

My recommendation to Alex is to identify a very simple and small database, a very complex and large database, and one in the middle. For each of these databases, Alex can do a detailed work breakdown analysis to estimate what it will take to migrate to the new release. Next, he will look at the entire population of databases and categorize them into similar groups of complex, medium, and simple. This may require some help from the other members of the DBA staff (it doesn't matter whether a few are misplaced, since it will not materially affect the overall estimate). Then, he just needs to multiply the number of complex databases by the estimate required to convert one, and do the same with the medium and small categories. Finally, he will total up the time for database conversion, add the time required for project management, and add an additional percentage for estimating contingency. The numbers might look like the following table:

Alex's Estimating Table

	Effort to Convert One Database	Approximate Number of Databases This Size	Total Effort
Small	8	55	440
Medium	15	112	1,680
Large	20	34	680
Total Conversion Effort		201	2,800
Project Management	15%		420
Subtotal			3,220
Estimating Contingency	10%		322
Total			3,542

When Alex is done, he will have a fairly scientific, defendable estimate for upgrading all 200-plus databases.

35 | Sean Makes a Guess and I Make a Prediction

STEP 3 MANAGE THE WORKPLAN

Tim started kindergarten the last week of August, and it was a very emotional time for all of us. Pam and I were worried Tim would have a hard time adjusting to school, and we were positive he would cry when we dropped him off on his first day. It turned out that Pam and I cried more than he did! It's tough watching your young child grow up, but it had not really hit us how much older he was getting until we watched him run away happily into the schoolhouse that first day.

I told my "sad-sack" story to Sean Robinson on Friday when I bumped into him in the parking garage at the end of the day. We were both sneaking out a bit early to get a jump on the weekend, and he was changing into a pair of tennis shoes behind his car. He was on his way to the gym for his nightly workout. I knew Sean was a bit of a health nut who enjoyed things like wheat germ and carrot juice. I was also told that he spent a lot of time at the gym, although I was not sure how much time "a lot" was.

"You sound like a real good father, Tom," Sean said after I finished my story. "I'm curious, though; do you find any correlation between raising a child and managing a project?"

We both laughed at the thought. When the laughter died down, I asked Sean about his project.

"I remember you said your project duration was about four months," I said. "You've been working for two-and-a-half months, right? Seems like you should be seeing the end."

"You've got that right," Sean said confidently. "We are about 60 percent complete."

When a project manager gives me a percentage complete figure for any project, it always sets off a little alarm in my head. Percentages are usually a sign of some guesswork. It's not a bad thing to give a high-level estimate of the percentage complete, but I decided to explore this answer a little more.

"Sixty percent complete?" I asked. "Is this a number your project management software generates?"

"No. But it's my estimate of where we are."

"Sean, when you and I met before, you had a good workplan that laid out the work to be completed. What's the workplan look like now?"

"Unfortunately it is not in as good a shape as it needs to be. We have been so busy lately I haven't even had time to update it."

"Well then, let me make a prediction," I said. "I predict your project will miss its deadline, because I don't think you know exactly how much work is remaining."

LESSON 35

KEEP YOUR WORKPLAN UP TO DATE THROUGHOUT THE PROJECT

Everyone has heard the old adage "Plan the work, and then work the plan." It's a clever phrase and it is actually quite true. There is huge payback to the project if you first spend quality time defining the work and building a workplan. This makes sure you know what you are doing and you know how to get the work done.

The second part is important as well. You must work the plan. This means you must actually follow the workplan, since it is your guide to completing the project.

This is the part that many project managers forget. The "plan the work, work the plan" cycle must be repeated throughout the project. It makes sense because you never know all of the details when you start a project. You cannot foresee or control every possible event when the work is in progress. So, the best-guess workplan that you used to start the project will need to be modified over time.

There are two reasons to update your workplan. First, you need to validate the work completed and compare it to the work that is scheduled for completion. This gives you a sense of whether you are ahead, behind, or on schedule. Knowing where you are against your schedule allows you to put corrective plans in place if necessary. If you end up trending over your deadline date, you have much more flexibility if you catch the trend as early as possible.

The second reason for updating the workplan is to review the remaining work and to verify that you still understand the work required to complete the project. The nature of the project can change over time, especially if it is a large one. Scope changes are added, issues are resolved, new risks are identified, the communication needs of the stakeholders may change, etc. The project manager must review the remaining work on a regular basis and ensure it is still an accurate reflection of the expected path to the completion of the project. If it is not, then the workplan can be modified to reflect a better path to completion.

The duration of Sean's work is four months, and his workplan may not need the rigor of a multimillion-dollar project. However, he should still update his workplan every week. In fact, his workplan should have a weekly, one-hour activity assigned for him to update the workplan. If his workplan is not kept up to date, he really does not know where he is on the project and what work is remaining to complete the project. It will be pure luck if his original workplan still reflects a valid path to completion.

When you ask project managers how their project is progressing, it is very common for them to give you a percentage complete. They are just trying to provide a sense for the amount of work completed and the amount remaining. There is nothing wrong with that.

However, if necessary, project managers must also be able to show where their project is on the workplan, as well as the series of activities remaining to complete the work. Project managers may need to go over this level of detail with a team member, or with their manager. If a project starts to experience problems, or starts to go over its budget and deadline, there may be a number of people who will suddenly become interested in going over the workplan in some level of detail. Of course, I am also one of the people interested in seeing an up-to-date workplan. When Sean said he was 60 percent complete, it was worth the follow-up questions from me to verify whether the estimate was based in fact, or based on guesswork.

In general, not updating the workplan is simply the result of a lack of discipline. Sean probably thinks he is too busy on project-related activities to keep up on the project management activities. This is usually short-sighted and will probably end up putting his team in a time crunch when they realize, towards the end of the project, just how much work remains to be completed. Sean absolutely must update his workplan and keep it up to date. He may or may not end up meeting his project deadline, but the best way to know ahead of time is to update the workplan and ensure the remaining activities and estimates are accurate.

36 Lindsay Wishes for a Problem-Solving Magic Wand

Lindsay Peterson stopped by my office in the first week of September to talk about her project to consolidate worldwide product sales for the Sales Department. I was trying to remember the last time I had spoken to her in an "official" capacity, but was having trouble remembering. I knew it had been awhile. After several minutes of thinking, I remembered it was the beginning of the year, shortly after the birth of her daughter Patricia. The Petersons lived just a few miles from Pam and I, and we often bumped into them at the local park, or at the supermarket. Lindsay was a good project manager and did not often ask for counsel. I knew something big must have happened for her to visit with me.

"Come on in Lindsay! How is Patricia doing these days?"

"She's doing great. Still just as tiny and cute as can be. I still can't believe how different things are with her around."

"Well, just remember not to take any of this time for granted. You know, Pam and I took Tim to kindergarten last week. They grow up so fast."

"Believe me, I know. We're trying to take every day as it comes and enjoy the time as much as possible. We're definitely giving the camera a workout!"

"That's funny," I said as Lindsay sat down in the chair in front of my desk. "So let's talk about your project. Have you encountered a hurdle?"

"That's why I came to see you. We've run into a major problem," she began honestly. "A new software component that is part of our system does not work with the version of the Web browser our company uses. The vendor component requires the new, updated browser version. We were initially told by our intranet support group that our company was going to migrate to this newer browser, but now the upgrade has been put on hold for at least three months."

"Hmmm. What have you done so far?"

Lindsay gave me a little history. "First of all, our testers raised this as a problem as soon as they realized the implications, and I notified our sales client right away. After initially being upset, they became engaged in the resolution process and we started looking for alternatives. First, we tried to get a version of the component that would run with the current browser, but the vendor does not have one. This is a new product for them, and they are not supporting older browser versions. Then we asked about upgrading the browser for our clients earlier than scheduled, but we were told we couldn't, since many other applications have not been tested with the new browser release yet. Then we talked to the client about removing the functionality the component provided, but they said the currency conversion calculations wouldn't work without it. We've looked at everything we can think of, but we must be overlooking something. What else should we be doing?"

"Have you met with your team and your client to brainstorm other alternatives and impacts?" I asked.

Lindsay was already ahead of me. "That's what we did first. Based on that meeting, we identified the alternatives that I have already mentioned. There are others we have looked at as well."

I thought for a second. "Lindsay, let me give you some bad news. The issues management process will help facilitate problem resolution, if there is a good alternative to apply. However, it sounds like the options you have remaining are bad ones. At this point, you need to work with your client to make the best of a bad situation."

"In that case, let me ask you a favor," Lindsay said with a straight face. "Can I borrow your magic wand for a minute? I just want to make this project disappear."

LESSON 36

USE ISSUES MANAGEMENT TO HELP CHOOSE THE BEST OF BAD ALTERNATIVES

Issues are major problems that impede the success of a project. They cannot be resolved without outside help. Usually, when problems arise on a project, there are some alternatives that will solve the problem or help you to implement a workaround. In many cases a number of viable solutions are available. You just need to find the best one. Sometimes a solution will end up costing money and time. Sometimes a solution doesn't cost you anything other than the time you spend resolving it. Applying good issues management techniques will help you to identify and focus on the problem until it is resolved. There are a number of good problem solving techniques that will help you to identify the cause, alternatives, and the best solution. Some examples of problem solving techniques include

- Pareto diagrams, which help identify the 80/20 rule. These help you focus on identifying the 20 percent of the causes that are causing 80 percent of the problems.
- "What-if" analysis, which helps you determine what the impact would be of solving certain aspects of the problem.
- Root cause analysis, which guides you through a series of "why" questions until you find the actual cause of the problem.

Although proactively managing issues gives you the best chance to resolve them in a timely manner, the process does not guarantee success. Let's review Lindsay's situation. First, a team member raised a problem as soon as it was discovered. Lindsay realized this problem was outside her team's ability to resolve, so she raised it as a formal project issue. She was able to get her client engaged in the resolution process. The entire team met to look at alternatives and came up with a prioritized list of potential solutions.

So far, Lindsay has done everything correctly. She has followed a good issues management process. However, the process has not resulted in an acceptable resolution. Some of the potential solutions are not possible, and some of the solutions are not acceptable to one or more of the major stakeholders.

Looking back, Lindsay might have helped herself out by identifying this as a potential risk earlier in the project. Since the vendor has a new product that only works with a newer version of the Web browser, this may have surfaced as a risk Lindsay could have monitored much earlier. She may have taken a different approach to the problem if she had kept an eye on it. However, Lindsay did receive initial assurances the Sales Division would be migrating to the newer browser on an earlier date, so she did not feel this was a major risk at the time.

At this point, Lindsay needs to take one more look at whether there are any other ideas to resolve this successfully. If not, she and the client have no alternative but to identify the best solution causing the fewest problems. Perhaps the worst case scenario will be to stop (or to pause) the entire project until the situation is resolved. There might also be options to perform some work manually, or to delay some features until the browser is upgraded. They might also try escalating the problem to senior management to see if they can get the priority raised on the browser upgrade. In any case, the client is not going to be happy with the outcome. At this point, the best alternative may be the one that inflicts the least pain and damage. It would be nice if every problem could be resolved by invoking a process, but sometimes it just doesn't work out that way.

37

Terri and Sarah Propose Half-Measures

Terri Milner and Sarah York stopped by my office to discuss a short project they had been assigned to. Terri and Sarah were sorority sisters in college who had recently been reunited when Sarah relocated to Dickens and began working at Mega Manufacturing in July. Terri had been with the company five years in June, and was generally respected for her intelligence, but somewhat criticized for her organizational skills, or lack thereof. They were both very outgoing, and I was sure they were enjoying the opportunity to work together, even if the project assignment was out of the ordinary. The two had been asked to put metrics in place to measure the overall satisfaction of the Manufacturing Department users when they call the IT help desk. Terri gave me some background about why the effort was underway, while Sarah twirled her pen in her hand.

"Tom, you know we just installed our manufacturing software at the new plant," Terri began. "We expect there will be problems whenever a new package goes in. However, it's September and there still seems to be an unusually large number of problems on this installation. The IT team has resources dedicated to getting the bugs ironed out, but we could be dealing with a high number of support calls for many months. The problems are currently all over the board, and they are not sure what to expect next."

"I see," I replied. "It sounds as if your client wants to get more information on the impact that these problems are having on their staff."

"You're right. The plant manager is not happy with the problem resolution process," Sarah jumped in. "Since the plant is located outside the corporate environment, they have difficulties getting calls logged in the help desk. They think they are waiting too long for return calls and they are also not happy with the resolution of many of the problems. They think the same problems are occurring over and over again."

"What does the help desk say?" I asked, not sure whom to direct the question to.

"Actually, this gets at one of the primary reasons for setting up the metrics process," Terri explained. "The help desk and the IT support group think they are responding in a timely manner. They say they have beefed up the staffing to help respond to the needs of the plant. However, no one knows for sure because we don't have any quantifiable numbers."

When people can't agree on what is perception and what is reality, it can cause problems trying to find the causes. However, this time it appeared all the groups were simply looking to verify the facts so that proper decisions can be made. The help desk, IT support team, and the plant manager were all supportive of this effort.

"You were asked to define a set of metrics and see how best to capture them." I recapped to Terri and Sarah. "What are you proposing so far?"

Terri gave me the initial list. "We want to collect information on the time that it takes to reach a live person on the help desk, on the time that it takes until an initial follow-up call from the support group is received, and on the time that it takes to resolve the problem. We also want to collect client survey metrics on the professionalism, knowledge, and courtesy of the help desk and support people."

"That sounds like a great start," I agreed. "But you might be missing an additional set of metrics that are even more important."

LESSON 37

COLLECT METRICS THAT CAN LEAD TO FUNDAMENTAL IMPROVEMENTS

Three major groups are collaborating on this project—the help desk, the IT support team, and the manufacturing plant manager. All of them are interested in getting more facts about the IT-related problems coming out of the new plant, and on the process that will help to resolve them in a timely manner. They are all frustrated because they don't have a common set of perceptions. The IT support team and the help desk say they have increased their capabilities to help the plant when problems arise. The plant management and staff think they are not getting a timely enough response. So, they are all partnering to come up with some facts to help make decisions.

On the surface, the metrics Terri and Sarah are proposing look fine. In fact, there is nothing wrong with them. The metrics they have identified so far provide a sense of the service level of the help desk and the IT support staff. The plant manager wants to be sure his people's problems are being resolved in a timely manner, and the proposed metrics will certainly give him better information in that area.

The question is whether these metrics get at the root causes of the problems the client is experiencing. In other words, Terri and Sarah are not proposing any metrics to provide insight into the causes of the problems. They are only proposing to measure how fast the problems are resolved once they have been reported to the help desk. Of course, the client wants problems resolved quickly, but what he really wants is not to have problems to begin with.

Let's assume that if valid statistics were available today, then they might show that the client was reporting 50 problems per week, with an average resolution time of 24 hours. If the focus is only on turnaround time, you can image, in time, that the average response time might be lowered to 12 hours. This would certainly be a better situation for the client. However, if there are still 50 problems reported per week, the client is still going to be dissatisfied.

Likewise, if the help desk and IT support team are courteous and professional, they would both be ranked highly in those client satisfaction metrics. If, however, the plant continues to report 50 problems per week, will the plant staff really be more satisfied? Probably not.

From the client's perspective, other root cause metrics should be gathered as well. Some examples include

- The number of problems reported per day and per week
- The number of problems identical to problems previously reported
- The types of problems grouped into categories, for further root cause analysis
- The severity of the problems (focus on eliminating major problems, then medium, then minor)
- The impact of the problems, in terms of lost hours

My advice to Terri and Sarah is to keep the metrics they are proposing to collect, but also to talk to the three groups about adding more metrics to show root causes and client impact. There is an old saying, "What gets measured gets done." If Terri and Sarah focus exclusively on the response times, the tendency will be for everyone to focus exclusively in that area. Although important, their goal should be to reduce the number of problems, the severity of the problems, and the impact of the problems to the client. In addition to that primary focus, they should also collect their proposed metrics to ensure that when a problem arises, it is resolved as quickly and painlessly as possible.

38

John Is the "Risk Eliminator," but Does He Need to Be?

A cold chill was starting to blow into Dickens, and I knew the fall season was starting to take shape. The leaves on the oak trees outside my office window were beginning to turn orange and red, and short-sleeve shirts were starting to be replaced by light turtlenecks and long-sleeve sweaters. The NFL was already in its third week, and Pam was starting to wonder what costume to buy Tim for Halloween. It was still just the third week of September, but people's minds were starting to turn to thoughts of winter, Thanksgiving, and Christmas. John Santos was no exception. He had asked me to come by his office on Wednesday afternoon around 3 p.m. to provide final feedback on his Project Definition.

"Tom, I can't believe I saw a store putting up Christmas decorations last night. I tell you, Christmas comes earlier and earlier every year," he said with a chuckle as I came into his office.

"Actually, it is December 25th every year," I replied with a straight face. After a few seconds I smiled and we both laughed. John's Project Definition was, all in all, a pretty good document, although I did want to talk to him about his risk plan. He was responsible for a project involving a major office move at our headquarters. A couple of business units had recently reorganized, and the inevitable follow-up had people moving to reflect the new organization charts.

"John, I see you have identified a number of risks to the project," I noted. "For each risk, you have also identified a plan to try to eliminate it. However, the move is not for three months. Given the timeline, I wonder whether there might be more sensible alternatives to some of your risk plans."

"There are a number of potential risks with a project this large," John replied. "The moving logistics are complex, and everything needs to happen in a sequence. If one move gets delayed, the entire schedule gets pushed back."

"I understand how interdependent everything is," I sympathized. "However, let's look at some of the risk plans. For instance, your moving company may end up on strike, so you are proposing engaging another company instead. This is a new company you have not used before."

"Yes," John agreed. "If our standard moving contractor is on strike, we need to have an alternative in place."

"You are also planning for a high volume of calls from people who need some minor tweaking after the move," I noted. "You plan to have your staff work paid overtime on nights and weekends to deal with this demand."

John spoke proudly. "This may cost us a bunch of overtime pay, but we are going to keep our service level up by responding to all requests within 48 hours."

"I see where you are going with your risk plans," I summed up. "However, there are a number of responses to perceived risks. You are trying to mitigate, or eliminate each risk. Let's discuss some alternatives and see if they are applicable instead."

LESSON 38

EVALUATE ALL RISK RESPONSE OPTIONS IN THE RISK PLAN

Since risks are generally perceived as bad, it makes sense for the first instinct of a project manager to be one that seeks to mitigate them. Mitigation should result in the elimination of the risk, or in the reduction of the chance that the risk event will occur. However, there are a number of other options for responding to a risk, including

- *Leave it:* This option works if you can, in fact, live with the result of the risk event occurring, or if the cost of other approaches is prohibitive. You may leave a risk alone if nothing can be done about it, even if the project may need to be cancelled if the event occurs.

- *Monitor the risk:* You may have enough time to monitor the risk to see if it will go away. The project manager creates a risk plan in the future only if the risk appears likely to occur.

- *Avoid the risk:* You may be able to isolate and avoid the condition causing the risk. For instance, if part of the project has high risk associated with it, you may be able to eliminate that entire piece.

- *Move the risk:* In some instances, the responsibility for managing a risk can be removed from the project by assigning the risk to another entity or third party. The third party may have specific expertise in that area, and can absorb any associated risks.

Notice that none of these options include ignoring the risk. Even the option to leave the risk is the result of a conscious decision.

In John's case, he is choosing to mitigate all of the identified risks. However, I asked him to be open to other options as well. For instance, let's look at the risk of a strike at the moving contractor. John has three months until the move, and he may not want to make any major changes now, such as developing a business relationship with a new company. Perhaps the best approach is to monitor this risk for the next 30 days. If the labor contract is renewed, then he will not need to make any changes at all. If a strike still seems imminent, then he will still have two months to put new plans into place. There is risk associated with using a new vendor on an important move like this. John probably doesn't want to make a change unless he has to.

John is also proposing heavy overtime so his service level will not drop after the move is complete. Again, this may be the best approach, but it may not. He should talk to his manager and major clients about another option—leaving the risk alone. After a major move, people understand there is going to be some disruption in service levels. He may be able to reset expectations for a short-term time frame. For instance, perhaps turnaround time for problems will be five days instead of two days. In other words, this may be a situation the company can live with, and may not require him to incur the expense of paid overtime.

John's risk plans were not wrong. In fact, these may be the best alternatives given what he knows today. However, a number of options are available for risk response. In general, risk response is based on the severity of the risk, the time frame when the risk event may occur, and the options available to you. For instance, if you have risk events occurring many months in the future, it may not make sense to jump right into risk mitigation activities. A lot can change over time. The project manager should look at all the appropriate risk response options, and the risk plans should be evaluated periodically to ensure they continue to address each threat appropriately.

39 | Nikki and Her Client Have Mismatched Expectations

I was unusually slow during the last week of September, so I decided to proactively check in with several project managers who I knew had projects in the works, to see if I could offer any assistance. My first meeting was with Nikki Hooper, who was working with her client to update an application on how commissions are paid. Nikki was a mother of three with short blonde hair and green eyes. An extremely conservative woman, Nikki was active on her church board as well as her school's Parent Teacher Association. This was my first interaction with her, and I could tell she was skeptical about whether or not I could offer any real advice or help. Like many people I have worked with in my role as project management advisor, she also appeared nervous, thinking that my true function was to assess her performance and competence as a project manager, and to determine whether she was someone worth keeping at Mega Manufacturing. I addressed this misconception first.

"You know Nikki, a lot of people think my job is to evaluate project managers," I began. "This could not be further from the truth. I was brought in to help project managers like you do their job more professionally and more effectively."

"Thanks for saying that up front, Tom," she replied. "I was a bit nervous after receiving your call, because I thought perhaps you had heard something bad about my project. I actually thought my client might have called to complain."

"Not at all. But why is your client complaining? Why don't you fill me in and let's see if I can help."

"Well, I am really having a problem right now trying to manage client expectations," she began. "Our business clients aren't being realistic. They want to completely automate the commission payment process and allow the salespeople to view information through the Web. We can't do everything they want because we are dealing with enhancements to a legacy system with a lot of older technology. We would have to completely rewrite it if we

did everything they wanted. I would love to hear your advice on how to better manage their expectations."

"Managing expectations can be tough," I replied, still trying to put her at ease. "But the place to start is the Project Definition. Did you write one for this project?"

"No, we didn't," she said. "We didn't think we needed one for an enhancement."

"How about business requirements?" I asked. "Do you have anything formally approved coming out of your analysis?"

"We met with the clients to gather their requirements, but we don't have much formally documented."

I paused for a few seconds. "Well, you asked me for advice on how to better manage the expectations of your client," I began. "The problem is you and your client never had an agreement on what your project was going to produce. You can't manage expectations effectively unless you have common expectations to begin with."

LESSON 39

GAIN A COMMON UNDERSTANDING FIRST TO EFFECTIVELY MANAGE CLIENT EXPECTATIONS

Managing expectations is one of the biggest challenges facing project managers. It seems as if your client always wants more than you can deliver, for less cost and effort than it really takes. This mismatch of expectations is one of the primary reasons projects do not end successfully. In many cases, the project team has one level of expectations for what the project will produce, but the sponsor and clients have another. The challenge for the project manager is to keep these expectations synchronized with the sponsor.

If you were to create a process for managing client expectations on a project, it would look something like this:

- *Establish an agreement:* This is probably the most overlooked, yet obvious part of the process. It is difficult or impossible to manage client expectations if you do not have some agreement to begin with.

- *Manage scope change:* Once an agreement is reached, changes should be managed through the scope change management process. This ensures the client and the sponsor approves all changes and helps to keep expectations in line.

- *Deliver against the expectations:* Again, this may seem obvious. However, once an agreement has been put into place, you need to make sure you deliver the work as expected.

- *Communicate proactively:* Communicate proactively through the status reporting process or as part of a broader Communication Plan. This helps the business client and the sponsor to keep up to date on progress, issues, risks, etc.

- *Periodically assess performance:* The project manager needs to monitor the work to ensure that the client commitments are met.

- *Reset expectations if necessary:* If the project manager feels the team is unlikely to complete the project according to the agreement, immediate steps should be taken to determine a new course of action and reset expectations with a modified agreement.

- *Complete the agreement:* Review the completed work with the client to ensure the terms of the agreement have been fully met. If not, negotiate what will be required to fulfill the agreement.

Given this simple process for managing expectations, it's no wonder Nikki is having trouble keeping client expectations in line with hers. After all, she never had a formal agreement with the client on the definition of the work (scope, objectives, risk, deliverables, etc.) to begin with. Nor did she set a common expectation as to the features and functions that would be delivered (business requirements). It's not surprising, then, that the client has "unrealistic" expectations as to what will be delivered.

Nikki will not be able to manage expectations effectively until she gains a common understanding of the work with her client. Since the project is well underway, it's probably too late to go all the way back to the Project Definition. However, she can go back and document the business requirements. Once the requirements are on the table, she can provide effort and cost estimates. When the sponsor sees that some of the requirements are prohibitively expensive to implement, they should agree to concentrate on those areas of the project that offer reasonable and cost-effective delivery. Until then, Nikki will always have a hard time managing the work because she has no agreement on what will be delivered.

40 | Alex's Project Is in Good Shape— Maybe

The first week of October brought cold winds and rain to Dickens, as well as numerous calls and e-mails for project management advice. I knew the next few months would be busy leading up to the end of the year, and my calendar was filling up fast.

I had just returned from a set of back-to-back-to-back-to-back meetings, when I received a panicked phone call from Jerry asking me if I could spare 20 minutes and swing by the large conference room on the third floor at the end of the day. I had to reschedule a late meeting with Alex, but I told Jerry I could make it.

As I approached the conference room at 5 p.m., I saw Jerry outside the main door.

"Hey, Jerry. What's up?" I asked as I approached the conference room.

"Tom, I know you hate surprises, but happy birthday!"

Just then the conference room door swung open to reveal several people in birthday hats and a big cake on the conference table. I was not sure if anyone would know it was my 40th birthday, but apparently the word had gotten out. Mega Manufacturing is a big company, so birthdays are traditionally celebrated internally by team members. Since I was really just a team of one, I had assumed that I would not be having a birthday celebration. It was nice to know that people remembered me. I blew out the candles on the cake and grabbed the first piece.

After several minutes of socializing, I noticed Alex in the back corner eating a piece of cake. I went over to see him.

"Hey Alex! I feel bad about canceling our appointment for a social function. I honestly thought Jerry was in trouble on his project."

"No need to explain, Tom. Jerry actually called me early this morning and let me in on the secret. If you don't mind, perhaps we can still talk briefly about my project. I could use your help with something."

"Why don't you update me on your project? How's it going?"

"Well, I think we are in pretty good shape," he said. "We have a number of changes to make to the database environment, but the work is not necessarily complex. It's just that we have a couple hundred databases to upgrade and it takes time."

"It sounds like a challenge," I agreed. "You said you thought you were in good shape. Does that mean you are on schedule or ahead of schedule?"

"I think we are on target," he said with a slight hesitation. "But, to be honest, I would have a hard time telling you precisely. We have many of our database administrators working on this project full time or part time. If one of them has some free time, they are jumping ahead to the next database upgrade. If they have other problems come up, they may not work on the upgrade for a number of days. So, some of them are ahead of schedule and some are behind. It's hard to figure out exactly where we are at any single point in time."

We talked for a few minutes about how he was tracking accomplishments. I did not have a major concern with how Alex was running the project, but I did see a problem with being unable to note exactly where he stood against his schedule.

"Let's talk some more about your workplan," I said to Alex. "You look like you have planned the project well, and it appears you are assigning work effectively. I think you need to set up some schedule milestones so you can better judge how your project is doing against your plan."

| LESSON 40 |

USE MILESTONES IN THE WORKPLAN TO TRACK OVERALL PROGRESS

Milestones are inserted into the workplan to signify the completion of a major deliverable or a major set of deliverables. They have zero duration. That is, they do not specifically require any work or effort to complete. However, they signify the project has passed a threshold.

Milestones are especially of interest to managers and sponsors, since they can provide a high-level snapshot of how you are tracking against your project workplan. For instance, you may add a milestone at the end of the analysis phase to signify the completion of the business requirements. Your sponsor and other stakeholders can just track the status of the project against the milestone date, without needing to understand the more detailed activities required. If you hit your milestone date, the assumption is the work is on track from a schedule perspective.

Milestones also provide the opportunity for a project management checkpoint. At every milestone, project managers can

- Evaluate previously identified risks to ensure they are being managed well.
- Look for new risks to the project.
- Verify that they have business commitment to continue.
- Verify that the project assumptions are still valid.
- Double-check the budget and deadline estimates to determine if they are still correct.

After carrying out these types of project management validation, you can plunge ahead with the next major part of the project.

Usually when you are managing a project, many (or most) of the activities follow a sequential pattern. For example, major analysis is followed by design, which is typically followed by construction, testing, and finally implementation. In most cases, the project manager can insert a milestone at the end of each of these project stages. However, on Alex's project, the activities are scheduled more arbitrarily, and don't necessarily follow a logical pattern. The timing of the work is based as much on team member availability as anything else.

In spite of the scheduling difficulty, or perhaps because of it, Alex needs some milestones to gauge his progress. For example, he could set up milestones at the completion of the database upgrades for each business unit, or perhaps milestones can be set after every 25 databases are converted.

The funny thing about Alex's project is he has done a very good job of building his workplan, and is managing the workplan well. In spite of that, he is nervous about whether he really understands if he is ahead or behind schedule. This is always a cause for concern because project managers should always know how they are trending against their workplans. If they don't, there is a good chance they could be behind schedule and not realize it until too late. Establishing milestones will allow Alex to focus on how the work is progressing.

In a simplistic sense, when a milestone arrives, Alex can see whether all the work up to that point is complete. If it is, then he is on or ahead of schedule. If some work is ahead of schedule and some behind schedule (which sounds like what is happening on Alex's project), he can shift available resources to overdue work so the project can catch up with the planned schedule. At that point, he can confirm all the work required up to that milestone is completed. He should also have some sense of whether the project is ahead of or behind schedule based on knowing the date the milestone was scheduled to be completed, the date it actually was completed, and the amount of work (if any) that has been completed ahead of schedule based on the milestone date.

Establishing milestones will provide Alex with checkpoints he can use to validate whether his project is progressing well against the schedule or whether corrective action is required.

41

Sean "Errors" by Not Managing Quality Early

Sean Robinson scheduled another meeting with me for the second week of October, and I was curious to see how he was doing on his project to track response rates for direct mail campaigns. The last time I saw him was in the parking lot after work as he was heading to the gym. When I saw him this morning in his office, it was clear he had just come from the gym as his gym bag was on the floor next to his desk, and he had that "just showered" look. I didn't know much about Sean, but I knew he took his physical well being very seriously.

"How many times do you work out a day, Sean?" I asked in a teasing tone as I sat my coffee mug down on the corner of his desk. I did not expect he would be working out more than once a day.

"Usually just once, either in the morning or after work. If I'm really motivated I go both times!"

"Wow, that sounds pretty intense. I'm lucky to get in one workout every other day."

"Well, it just takes discipline, Tom. I'd be happy to meet you in the gym every day, either before or after work. We can work out together, and I'll get you started on a diet and exercise program that will make you feel great!"

I knew I was getting in over my head. "I'm not sure I can commit the time right now, but I'll get back to you on it," I replied, trying not to sound too uninterested. "Tell you what, let's exercise our brains a bit this morning."

We both chuckled. It had been a month or two since we last spoke, so if Sean was on track, his project should be winding down about now.

"We're getting to the end," Sean said, shifting his weight. "But the user acceptance testing is taking longer than expected. I guess that's good and bad. It's bad that it is taking more time than expected, but on the positive side, the more errors we catch in testing, the higher the quality of the final solution."

Sean's mention of the "higher quality of the final solution" intrigued me. "What kind of errors are you catching?" I asked.

"Our users are being very thorough—they are catching all kinds of errors. Most are in the interfaces between the various subsystems. Some are programming logic errors. A couple of the worst problems were caused by some screwups in the original requirements. Those have taken quite a bit of time to correct." Sean began stretching his legs.

"It's great your users are catching all these errors. But did you perform any quality reviews or get any user signoffs on your work as it was originally being completed?"

"No, we didn't," Sean said chuckling. "We probably should have done more things like that. But it seemed like we didn't have the time."

"It seems like you do have the time," I countered. "You're just spending it now instead of earlier in the project. In fact, I'll bet you are spending more time fixing problems now than you would have spent avoiding them earlier."

LESSON 41

ESTABLISH PROCESSES TO CATCH ERRORS AS EARLY IN THE PROJECT AS POSSIBLE

Everyone has heard the saying, "You don't have time to do it right, but you do have time to do it twice." This means the incremental time required to validate the work is done correctly the first time is sacrificed, and you are then forced to spend extra time on rework and fixing problems at the end of the project. Our familiarity with the project life cycle has reached the point where we think we can rush through many activities in the project since we hope we will catch all the errors in testing. Unfortunately, it is not a one-to-one tradeoff, since the time it takes to fix problems is almost always more than the time required to prevent them to begin with.

Two main factors underpin the quality management process: build work processes that reduce errors to begin with, and find leftover errors as early in the project life cycle as possible.

The first aspect of reducing errors involves activities like training, checklists for deliverables, following proven standards, and reusing pre-built components. These are all investments in helping the team members create deliverables correctly the first time. If you train your team, for instance, in how to apply a new technology, you hope the team will be able to utilize the new technology correctly, and with a minimum of errors.

The second aspect of finding errors as early as possible includes activities like inspections, signoffs, and walkthroughs. For instance, misunderstandings and mistakes in deliverables and scope need to be found in the planning process. One way is to make sure the sponsor signs and approves the Project Definition. Likewise, errors in business logic need to be caught in the analysis phase. Design errors need to be caught in the design phase, and errors in constructing a solution need to be identified in the initial unit and integration testing.

The project manager should be aware that, in almost all cases, a good quality management process does require more effort hours and cost at the beginning of the project. However, these costs are more than offset by a reduction in the time needed to correct errors in the testing phase, or worse, when the solution goes into production.

The fact that Sean is catching so many errors at the end of the project is not a sign of a good quality solution. In fact, it may be an indicator of a lack of quality in the process used to build the solution. For instance, it would have been much less costly for Sean's team to have spotted problems with the business requirements during the analysis phase of the project, rather than having to fix the problems during user acceptance testing. These errors in requirements could have been uncovered simply by having the client formally approve the requirements. This is not to say the requirement would have then been perfect. It is always possible the client may have missed some of the important requirements needed for the project. However, having to formally approve the requirements would have forced the client to review this information more diligently. It would also have allowed Sean to invoke scope change management when these new requirements came up late in the project.

The other errors Sean mentions have to do with the testing process. The purpose of the client acceptance test is simply to validate that the solution works as expected. This is not the time to be catching interface errors and programming errors. Based on the fact that his team is finding these types of errors, it appears that both the programming process and the subsequent testing process had flaws. These types of errors should have been caught earlier and are a sign the testing process was not rigorous enough.

42

Danielle Has Satisfied All Her Clients—Except One

Mega Manufacturing offered its employees many great perks, but the one I enjoyed most was the cafeteria. The company contracted a catering firm in Chicago called Cool Eats to run the cafeteria, and the selection was stupendous. Every day you could pick items from a vast salad bar, deli, Chinese wok, American grill, and fruit stand. There was also an ice cream bar that I did not visit frequently, but every now and again it hit the spot. Usually, the pressures of work meant that I just grabbed a quick snack at my desk, but I would have liked to eat in the cafeteria more often. Today I was having lunch with Danielle Bartlett, so I would get to enjoy this benefit. I had just sat down after ordering a cheeseburger and fries from the grill when Danielle came over. Danielle was finishing up her second project since I first met her on Valentine's Day. Her latest project was to establish an intranet portal Web site that could be used to communicate more effectively between the Facilities Department and its numerous vendors.

"Looks good," Danielle said, eyeing my burger and fries as she sat her tray down. "Let me grab a soda and I'll be right back." Danielle had ordered a small salad and chicken soup, so I knew she must either be eating healthy or calming her stomach.

"Danielle, your lunch suggests your stomach might be bothering you. Are you stressed out about something?"

"You are very wise, Tom," she said with a smile. She said her project was going over budget and past its estimated end date. Her sponsor had just found out, and was not happy.

"Frankly, I am a little surprised," she began, sipping her soup. "I thought I was managing the project well. We developed a set of requirements for the installation of the estimating package, but as the project progressed, the users had new requirements they had forgotten to include in the initial stages of analysis. Whenever this happened, I initiated standard scope change management procedures."

"Tell me what your scope change procedures were," I replied. *"Perhaps they were missing some important piece."*

Danielle described the process to me. *"Whenever a scope change request was made, we documented it and created a cost estimate. Then we took the change to the client and verified whether the business benefit of the change was worth the cost and effort. If she said to go ahead, we proceeded. In fact, I have everything documented."*

"You'll need to explain to me why your sponsor is unhappy," I said. *"If you invoked scope change management, and the change was approved, the impact to the project should have been known."*

"The sponsor says she didn't approve the changes and she was not aware the project was going over budget," she replied. *"I guess we didn't do a good enough job of managing her expectations."*

Now I was really confused. *"I don't understand. I thought you said the sponsor approved all the scope changes?"*

"No, I said the client approved the changes," she explained. *"When a user requested a change we always went to their manager for approval. I thought if a manager approved the work, we should go ahead."*

"Now I see," I concluded. *"You have made the common mistake of not understanding the full role of the sponsor. There may be many people who are users and stakeholders, but the only person who can approve a change is the sponsor."*

LESSON 42

GAIN SPONSOR APPROVAL FOR SCOPE CHANGES REQUIRING BUDGET AND DEADLINE CHANGES

There are many people who have some level of interest in your project. The clients are the people in the organization(s) that the project is undertaken for. The end users are the people in the client organization who will actually use the products produced from the project. There are also many other stakeholders who have an interest in your project but don't specifically belong to the client organization. And, of course, there is the sponsor. The sponsor is the specific person who approved the project and is normally providing the funding.

It is natural for the project team to want to please their clients. However, this desire to be "client focused" often leads them to forget the main client of the project. The team most often works with the end users and their managers. The end users and their managers are typically the people who provide requirements, answer questions, and test the product to ensure it meets their needs. The end users are the people who will ultimately live with the final solution. Since these are the people the project team deals with the most, they are often considered to be the ultimate client. However, they are really the "little c" client.

When it comes to declaring success or failure, and when it comes to managing expectations, the sponsor matters most. And when you have to consider changing the budget or delivery date, the sponsor is the person with the power. The sponsor is the "big C" client.

Danielle thought she had a good scope change management process for her project. She was

1. Receiving scope change requests from end users

2. Documenting the requests

3. Estimating the impact of the changes to the project

4. Taking them to the client manager for approval

In reality, however, the client manager was really just verifying whether or not the change had business value. The client manager was not in a position to know whether the changes would impact the project deadline and budget.

All of this may have worked out okay if the project budget and deadline had not been compromised. However, these lower-level managers cannot make decisions requiring budget and deadline changes. They do not have authority to add to the project budget. In these instances, only the sponsor can make the decisions. Of course, the sponsor may delegate this role to another person for day-to-day items. In that case, the sponsor designee would be the only one to make these types of decisions.

Danielle and I had a good discussion on this point. The good thing was she was trying to follow a good scope change process. However, she was not going to the right person to make decisions that had an impact on the budget or deadline. The client manager may have thought the changes were important, but she did not have the authority to approve additional time or budget. The sponsor needs to do that. So now Danielle finds herself in an uncomfortable position. In her desire to be client focused, she has upset the client that matters most—the project sponsor.

43

Lindsay Has a Halloween Fright— Her Project Is Behind Schedule

Lindsay Peterson stopped by my office on Halloween day to discuss her project to consolidate worldwide sales data for the Sales Department. I hardly recognized her when she stepped into my office. She was wearing a white jumpsuit, with big gold glasses and a fake wig. Mega Manufacturing encouraged its employees to come dressed in costumes for Halloween, and Lindsay's was one of the best—a female Elvis!

"Boy, it's tough to imagine the teenagers swooning over you," I joked as she came in and sat down.

"Very funny, Tom. Tell me, who exactly are you suppose to be?"

I was wearing a regular suit and tie, but had an old reporter's hat on, with glasses and an exaggerated parting in my hair. I stood up to provide a clearer clue as to my costume. I had purposely left the middle buttons on my dress shirt undone, and I pulled them aside to show Lindsay my blue T-shirt with a large "S" printed on it.

"Ah, Clark Kent. Very clever."

"What do you mean," I said in a deadpan voice. "I was just going to say that I am not wearing a costume today. Now tell me 'King,' what's got you in Heartbreak Hotel on your project?"

"Tom, you know we recently came up with a workaround to replace some Web reporting software that would not work with our browser," Lindsay started. *"Well, we are behind schedule. I wanted to get some tips from you on things we can do that might help."*

"Have you tried anything so far?" I asked.

"We have assigned a couple of new part-time people to the project," Lindsay noted. *"But they are not having much effect. At this point, we will probably end up missing our deadline. However, I want to prepare a new workplan and I want to see how close we can get to the original date."*

"Okay," I agreed, standing up to write on the whiteboard. "First, let's verify that your new part-time resources are working on the right activities. Then let's list out a number of techniques that will help to accelerate the schedule."

LESSON 43

BE PROACTIVE IN APPLYING TECHNIQUES TO ACCELERATE THE PROJECT SCHEDULE

The project manager starts off a project with a workplan. However, it seems projects never behave exactly as planned, and soon you need to make adjustments. Some activities end late and new ones are needed you didn't account for. If you are lucky, you have some activities completing early as well, and you have some built-in contingency to help absorb inaccurate estimates. However, if you are unlucky (this seems to be the case more often than not), you end up in a situation where you start trending over your deadline.

The first responsibility of the project manager is to understand the work remaining so you can catch this problem as early as possible. If you find you are trending four weeks behind schedule, for instance, it is better to understand that with six months to go rather than with two months to go. The earlier you recognize the problem, the more flexibility you have to resolve the situation.

After you realize you are trending past your deadline, you must also try to understand the cause(s). If you do not understand the cause of the problem, you may put a plan into place that fails because the problem continues to occur. Regardless of how you get there, you are obliged to get back on schedule if at all possible. If you cannot meet your committed deadline, you should strive to put together a new realistic estimate. However, you should also strive to complete the work as close to the original deadline as possible.

The following techniques can be applied to the situation. This list is not in order of priority, and some techniques may work better in certain situations, whereas others can be applied more successfully elsewhere. Some of these techniques may require additional funding, but that may be a viable option if the deadline date is more important to the client than the budget.

- *Work overtime:* Everyone hates it, but one logical solution to consider is overtime. If people work more hours, they can get more work done in the same amount of calendar time. Overtime may be the best option if you are close to the end of the project and just need a final push to get everything done on schedule. If you are toward the end of the project, you also may be able to give people time off after the project is completed. If you are still early in the project, there are probably other options that are more effective. There may be cost implications to this option if you need to have contract resources work overtime.

- *Reallocate resources onto the critical path:* The project manager must first understand what activities are on the critical path. After all, if the project is trending over deadline, by definition the critical path is late. Once the critical path is understood, you should see if resources can be moved from other activities to help the activities on the critical path. This will get the project back on track by delaying or stretching out some of the work that is not on the critical path. Be careful though—delaying some work may end up changing the critical path. Always make sure you double-check the critical path each time you change the schedule. Lindsay should explore this option in more detail. She has applied two part-time resources to the project with minimal results. It's possible they were assigned activities off the critical path. It is also possible they worked on the critical path, but as the path was shortened, a new critical path emerged.

- *Double-check all dependencies:* Schedule dependencies represent activities that must be executed in a certain order. Invalid dependencies make it appear activities must be performed sequentially, when they can really be done in parallel. For instance, if you are building a house, you cannot start putting up the frame until the foundation is poured and dried. If you are trending over your deadline, these dependencies should be revalidated, since it is possible the schedule is being lengthened by dependencies between invalid activities.

- *Check time-constrained activities:* Time-constrained activities do not change based on the number of resources applied. For instance, you may be allocating team members to a five-day class. The class takes five days if 1 person attends, and it still takes five days if 20 people attend. All of these time-constrained activities should be checked to verify the timeframe. Perhaps assumptions could be changed with a different approach. For instance, if you have to wait two days for concrete to dry, perhaps renting fans to blow on the concrete could shorten the time.

- *Swap resources:* One cause for trending over your deadline might be that one or more resources are not as productive as you originally planned. In some instances, you may be able to simply swap people who are working on different activities within your project. At other times, it may mean releasing a team member and bringing in another person. Remember, the activities on the critical path are key. You may have the option to assign a more productive resource to those activities, while reassigning a less-productive resource to noncritical path activities.

- *"Crash" the schedule:* Crashing the schedule means applying additional resources to the critical path to get the biggest schedule gain for the least amount of incremental costs. For instance, if one person were assigned to complete an activity in ten days, you could investigate whether two people could complete it earlier. If two people can complete the work in six days, you will have accelerated the schedule by four days, at an incremental cost of two work days (two people for six days versus the original ten-day estimate). You may be able to further crash the schedule by applying three resources. Perhaps now the activity would take four days, or four-and-a-half days. Typically, the more resources you throw at an activity, the higher the incremental cost will be, while you will receive less in incremental time savings.

- *Fast track:* Fast track means you look at activities normally done in sequence and assign them totally or partially in parallel. For instance, in my home building example earlier, I said the house frame could not be constructed until the foundation was dry. However, if the house is large enough, you may have options to fast track by starting to erect the frame on the side of the home where the foundation was poured first. The foundation will harden there first, and might allow you to erect the frame on that side, while the foundation on the far side of the home is still drying. Fast-tracking usually involves risk that could lead to increased cost and some rework later.

- *"Zero tolerance" scope change:* Many projects begin to trend over deadline because more work has been added than originally committed to. This could be a result of poor scope change management, or it could be that small changes are being worked in under the radar screen. However, if you are at risk of missing your deadline date, you must work with the client and team members to ensure absolutely no unplanned work is being requested or worked on—even if it is just one hour. All energy should go into accelerating the agreed upon core work.

- *Improve processes:* When you look at the cause of the project trending over schedule, you may find some of the internal work processes could be improved. You should solicit team member feedback and look for ways within your team's internal control to streamline processes. For instance, perhaps you have a daily status meeting that does not provide value and which can be scaled back to once per week. You may also find there are bottlenecks with getting deliverables approved that can be overcome through a different process.

- *Scope back the work:* One option is to look at the work remaining and negotiate with the sponsor to remove some of it from the project. If you feel some of the remaining work is not essential to the project, you could discuss eliminating it completely. If the remaining work is all essential to the solution, this discussion still might need to take place as a last resort. You may have some options to complete this project on time with less than 100 percent functionality, and then execute a follow-up project to complete the remaining requirements.

- *Improve morale:* Team members will work harder and perform better if they do not spend time complaining and sulking. You can build shared purpose, increased camaraderie, and do some fun things to get people excited and happy again.

It will take a discussion between Lindsay and her sponsor to determine which options are best for their project. If the deadline date for your project is important, the worst thing the project manager can do is to ignore the schedule overrun and just let things keep going as they are. There are many proactive techniques that can be applied to try to accelerate the schedule. Lindsay can have an intelligent discussion with the sponsor to look at the alternatives, how much each option will accelerate the schedule, and the incremental cost to the project (if any).

44 | Marty Has a Work Breakdown

Pam and I took Tim trick-or-treating on Halloween night until about 9:30 p.m. He picked out his own costume this year, settling on Buzz Lightyear from the Toy Story movies. His pumpkin-shaped bucket was nearly full when we got home, but he was so tired from walking around and carrying his bounty he quickly fell asleep on the couch. I was recounting the story of our night to Marty McKnight in her office the following afternoon, and she laughed when I told her about Tim falling asleep right away. Apparently her youngest daughter did the same thing.

"She enjoyed getting all dressed up as a ballerina, but she didn't particularly care for ringing doorbells and asking strangers for candy. By the time we got home, she could barely keep her eyes open," she said. Marty was in her late 20s, and had only a few years' experience in the Marketing Department of Mega Manufacturing.

"Why don't you bring me up to speed on your project, Marty?" I said.

"I am an analyst in the Marketing Department," Marty began. "As you know, we have been doing marketing campaigns for many years, and some are very successful. However, we have a new department head, and he wants us to revamp the traditional model we have for campaigns. He wants them to be developed sooner, to include a Web component, to appeal to younger customers, and for them to be backed up with more metrics that show their effectiveness. He wants more changes as well, but you get the picture."

"Loud and clear," I said. "It sounds like he wants to reengineer your overall model for conducting marketing campaigns."

"Yes, that's the word he used—'reengineering,'" Marty confirmed. "So, reengineering is an IT term, right? I thought I would come over and get some advice for how to put a game plan together. I'm not really sure how to begin."

"Well, 'reengineering' is not really an IT term," I noted, trying to sound competent without sounding too smart. "In fact, much of the common use of the term is in the context of business reengineering, which is exactly what you are trying to do. I have a technique to get you started on a new model. It's called a work breakdown structure."

LESSON 44

USE THE WORK BREAKDOWN STRUCTURE TECHNIQUE TO IDENTIFY ALL THE WORK REQUIRED FOR A PROJECT

Let's first understand exactly what it is that Marty is looking for. She has been asked to build a model that will describe how the Marketing Department will conduct campaigns in the future. This model is basically a workplan template. The model will describe what things you do to start a campaign, to determine the audience, to work with vendors, to analyze the market, to gather metrics, etc. You can easily imagine the result of Marty's effort will be a workplan template describing all of the activities required to create, launch, and track a marketing campaign.

The only thing unusual about her project is she has been asked only to create the workplan model. In most cases, you build your workplan, and then use it to execute a project. Marty is building a workplan template for other marketing teams to use after her.

One of the ways to begin building a workplan is with a technique called work breakdown structure (WBS). The WBS technique is especially helpful when you are not sure exactly what you are getting into. It is possible one person could create the WBS. However, that would imply one person has all of the knowledge, and that is typically not the case when the WBS technique is used.

The place to start, then, is by gathering a group of interested people, all with knowledge and expertise that they can bring along to solve the overall problem. The meeting can be facilitated, but it doesn't have to be. The session rarely starts with a blank slate. There is usually some preexisting information, such as goals, strategies, constraints, standards, etc., that help frame the overall solution. If you have a Project Definition, be sure to note the deliverables, assumptions, approach, etc. In Marty's case, for instance, the group can start by listing the stated requirements from the sponsor, such as including the Web, appealing to younger customers, executing faster, etc.

With a WBS technique, you are basically building an inverted tree. In other words, you are going to start at a high level and identify all of the more detailed activities that need to take place to complete that higher level. Let's take a closer look at the process.

First, determine what large chunks of work must be carried out for the entire project to be completed. At this point, how you define the first level of work does not matter. It is only important for all of the work to be identified at the end of the process. For instance, a marketing campaign might be initially broken up into steps such as "planning, analysis, design, build, rollout." The breakdown could also be by marketing medium, such as "television, radio, magazine, newspaper, Web, point-of-sale," etc. On the other hand, an IT application might have high-level deliverables such as "online application, data warehouse, datamarts, user query tools." Break down the work into whatever structure makes sense for your project. The initial high-level breakdown of work is called level 1. Remember, the point of the work breakdown structure is to capture all of the elements of the work. Sequencing is not important at this time.

After you finish your initial breakdown of the work, look at each of the level 1 components and see if they need to be broken down further. They should be broken down further if it is not clear what is required to complete the work or if the estimate to complete the work is greater than an estimating threshold—usually around 80 hours.

Look at these large pieces of work and determine all of the activities required to complete them. This gets you to level 2 of the work breakdown structure. When the process is complete, look at the lower level again to see if the underlying work is clear, concise, and can be done in 80 hours or less. Any activities that cannot are broken down further.

You continue to build the inverted tree for all lower-level activities, until all of the work is represented in as much detail as is necessary, with no activities having an estimated effort larger than your estimating threshold of 80 hours. This takes you to levels 3, 4, 5, and so on. It should be a rare case where you would need to break the work down greater than five levels.

My advice to Marty is to get a team of marketing people together and build a WBS that lays out the work they think should be done on future campaigns. The next step is to sequence all of the lowest-level activities (those that have not been broken down further). Then they should estimate the effort required to complete each activity within each sequence. If they can do those three things (WBS, sequencing, and effort estimate), then Marty should have the basic model for future campaigns to circulate for feedback and approval.

When a marketing campaign starts in the future, the campaign manager will use the plan as his or her model. The campaign manager can remove unnecessary activities, assign resources to the remaining activities, and estimate the effort and duration of each activity. The marketing campaign plan can then be executed.

45 Rick Thinks Our Status Reports Taste Like Stale Fish

When Wayne Moretti left Mega Manufacturing, I began reporting to Rick Goodall, a senior vice president. Rick was a great guy who fully supported the idea of a project management adviser and really saw the value of the position. He took me to lunch the day before Wayne left, and we've had a good working relationship ever since. He invited me to lunch the week of Thanksgiving to discuss status reports and to catch up on other business.

We decided to walk to Joe's Fishmarket, a newly opened restaurant about two blocks west of Mega Manufacturing. I had noticed that it had opened a few weeks ago, but I did not know anyone who had eaten there. I ordered the fish 'n' chips special and Rick tried the flounder. We started off talking about nonbusiness-related matters. As our lunch arrived, though, Rick passed along some feedback to me about status reporting.

"Tom, I've been hearing concerns from some of the senior managers about the quality of the information being reported in the project status reports," Rick said between bites of his french fries. "I need you to work with the project managers to make these more effective."

"What kinds of concerns are you hearing?" I asked.

"Some of the managers are receiving project status reports on a monthly basis," Rick explained. "However, these are just a bunch of words. After reading the reports, they still don't have a good understanding of the project status."

"Our company needs to move to a higher level on status reporting," I agreed. "A year ago, status reports were created sporadically, and everyone used a different format. Now every project manager does status reporting on a monthly basis in a consistent format. However, I agree that the information in the reports is not always at the high-quality level we need it to be."

"Great," Rick replied. "Let's figure out how to get the content improved over the next two monthly reporting cycles. By the way, how's your fish?"

"You know," I sighed. "The fish is a little stale and a little bland."

"Sounds like our status reports!" Rick shot back.

We both chuckled.

LESSON 45

WRITE YOUR STATUS REPORTS WITH THE READERS' INTEREST IN MIND

Is there a project manager out there who likes to do status reports? If so, I would like to shake his or her hand. Your team accomplishes great feats, solves perplexing problems, and strives to meet deadlines. Then, when the time comes to tell your managers and your clients about the status of the project, you want to spend as little time as possible providing the absolute minimum amount of information required. It might be understandable (but still not right) if the project was in trouble. But even project teams doing well don't always communicate effectively in the status report.

Of course, let's first also agree that management stakeholders and project sponsors need to be more involved in a project than just spending a few minutes a month reading a status report. If they do not feel they are getting the information they need, they can always pick up the phone (or even talk face to face) to get more information from the project manager. But project managers need to make life easier for them.

Project managers must come to terms with the fact that communicating status is one of their fundamental responsibilities. Communicating status is a way to manage expectations, and to keep everyone informed on how the project is progressing. Your managers and stakeholders have many priorities they are working on at any given time. The status report is one of the ways they can keep an eye on your project and know if they need to become more engaged.

The bottom line is the project manager must prepare the status report to meet the needs of the reader and not to see how few words can be included. The reader does not want to know all of the details of your project, so don't include them. The reader also does not want to read about how smoothly the project is progressing, if, in fact, there are problems. A good status report should include

- *Project recap:* This is usually in the form of a short opening paragraph that gives an overall summary of how the project is progressing. Sometimes, this recap is designed as a series of standard questions such as, Will the project be completed within its deadline date? and, Are issues being addressed and resolved in a timely manner? These types of opening questions provide a quick indication to the reader of whether there are problems with the project. If everything is going well, no further explanation is required. However, if there are problems, or if there are significant variations the reader should know about, they should be described next. For instance, if major scope change requests were approved, they should be noted here. If the project is behind schedule, this should be noted, as well as what is being done to get back on schedule. This recap section may be the most important, since it provides the overview of the project. You want your readers to read the entire status report. However, if they only read the recap section, they should still understand the overall status of the project. It is very common to include an overall color indicator that recaps the overall status. Green would indicate everything is fine. Yellow would point out that caution is required and that the project is at risk of missing its deadline or budget. A red indicator would mean that the project is already in trouble and will miss its budget, deadline, or both.

- *Major accomplishments:* This section provides insight into the significant work accomplishments from the prior reporting period. This is where the project manager must be careful to communicate in a manner the reader will understand. This section cannot be too technical, nor should it be so high level the reader has no perspective on what the accomplishments mean.

- *Major work planned for next period:* This is similar to the prior section, but it gives the reader a sense for the work coming up. Again, put this in a perspective the reader will understand.

- *Other information:* Other information important to the organization may be included here—for example, this could be other sections or attachments, such as budget reports, a Scope Change Log, or an Issues Log.

It is not easy to come up with the right combination of information that would be of interest to all readers. In fact, you may need a detailed status report for the stakeholders interested in your project, and then a higher-level summary status report for more senior managers interested in the project, but who don't have enough perspective and context to understand the details.

The bottom line is project managers should take pride in their status reports and try to provide relevant and clear information to their readers. If your readers are not clear on how the project is progressing, you have not done an effective enough job.

46 It's Magic! Lauren Sees an Assumption Turn into an Issue

Lauren Carter was a tall woman who had made a big name for herself locally playing basketball. She still ranked in the top ten for most career points in Illinois high school girls basketball history, and was one of the state leaders for most rebounds. She played high school ball in Dickens for Thomas Jefferson High School before moving on to college ball at the University of Illinois. She graduated with a degree in business and played a little professional basketball. However, the women's side of the sport was not as popular back then as it is today, and she ended up utilizing her business degree instead of her basketball skills in the workforce. She was a good project manager who gained a lot of respect at Mega Manufacturing from her peers. She called me Wednesday morning and asked to meet me that same day. When I met with her, it was clear right away a problem had developed.

Lauren was managing a project to make all the hard-copy reports supporting the factory floor available through the Web. The project was maybe two-thirds complete.

"Sounds like there's a problem with your project, Lauren. What's the latest?" I asked.

"Yes, we've got a big problem," she said, taking a deep breath. "We have been using the beta release of a Web reporting tool and it has worked pretty well. However, the vendor announced this morning they have been purchased by one of their competitors. The vendor is no longer sure they will bring this reporting tool to market, since the company purchasing them has a very similar product. This has really thrown a monkey wrench into our plans, and there is no question it will affect our project end dates. First, we will have to decide on a new tool and then retest everything. I wanted to talk to you about some ideas we have to resolve this. Each potential solution has some positives and negatives."

"I'm glad you at least have a couple of options for resolving the tool problem," I said. "Didn't you have a chance to see this possible outcome occurring?"

"When we started the project, we looked at the risk of using this vendor," Lauren replied, shaking her head. "However, the risk seemed low at the time. They have a good product and they were financially sound. So, we made an assumption they were going to work out okay. We did not see a need to include them in our risk management plan."

"Well," I said. "I'm sure that was the case when you started the project. But there has been some recent press about these two companies talking."

"Really," Lauren leaned back, a little surprised. "I guess we have not been keeping up on current events like we should."

LESSON 46

UPDATE YOUR RISK PLAN PERIODICALLY THROUGHOUT THE PROJECT

A risk assessment is one of the key project management processes performed in the initial project definition. The assessment includes the following steps:

1. Identify project risks. This includes understanding the risks inherent in any project with characteristics like yours, as well as brainstorming potential risks unique to your project.

2. Assign a risk level to each identified risk. The risk level should be high, medium, or low, depending on the severity of impact and the probability of the event occurring. For instance, a highly likely, high-impact event is obviously a high risk. On the other hand, a low-impact project risk that is likely to occur would be classified as a low risk.

3. Create a response plan for each high-risk event. The response plan for each risk should include the activities to manage the risk, with people assigned and completion dates. Remember, there are five major responses to a risk—leave it, monitor it, avoid it, move it to a third party, or mitigate it.

4. Evaluate the medium-risk events. Each of the medium risks should be evaluated to see if a response plan is needed. If the impact is severe enough, you probably want to create a response plan for them as well.

5. Look at any low-risk items and see whether they should be listed as assumptions. In this way, you recognize there is potential for problems, but because the risk is low, you are assuming the condition will not occur.

6. Move the activities associated with the risk response plans to the *project workplan*. Moving the activities to the workplan should help guarantee the work is actually completed and ensures that the workplan is the primary focus for all work planning and monitoring.

Lauren and her team did a good job on the initial risk assessment. However, they did not do well on the remaining two follow-up activities:

7. Monitor the risk response plan. Lauren needs to monitor the risk response plans to ensure they are being executed successfully. New activities should be added if it looks like the risk is not being managed successfully.

8. Periodically reevaluate risks. The risk assessment process needs to be repeated periodically throughout the project based on current circumstances. New risks may arise as the project is unfolding and some risks that were not identified earlier may become visible at a later date. This is also the time to validate the severity of known risk events. In addition, previously identified risk events may still be valid, but the likelihood or severity of the risk may have changed. This ongoing risk evaluation should be performed on a regular basis, say monthly, or at the completion of major milestones.

Lauren, like many other project managers, performed the initial risk assessment, but she did not perform the follow-up and ongoing risk management processes. Just as the workplan needs to be updated on an ongoing basis, so the risk plan needs to be double-checked as well throughout the project.

Lauren's team initially identified a risk with the software maker, but they felt the risk was low. Therefore, they assigned it to the level of an assumption. That was fine at first, but Lauren and her team did not go back and periodically update the risk plan. If they had reevaluated the plan, they would have looked at this low-level vendor risk. Had they reassessed the risk, there is also a good likelihood they would have seen the vendor was in acquisition talks. This knowledge would have allowed them to raise the risk level and focus some energy on looking at alternatives and contingencies.

If Lauren had upgraded this potential event from an assumption to a risk, the team would have had some time to deal with the situation. Of course, it does not mean the acquisition was more or less likely to occur. However, they could have considered alternatives, such as beginning to test the software of the acquiring company, or other software packages.

Now that the event has occurred, the situation is classified as an issue, and issues management techniques are utilized. The team may identify the same options for resolution as if they had done a risk plan earlier. However, if they had utilized a risk plan, they would have had time to prepare a plan of attack in case the event occurred. At this point, all they can be is reactive, and any resolution will probably have an impact on the timing of the project.

47 Sally May Be Squandering Her Good Fortune

The weeks between Thanksgiving and Christmas are traditionally slow times of the year at Mega Manufacturing. Many people take vacation time at the end of the year, and even if they don't, I find most people are ready for the Christmas break about two weeks before it arrives. As such, they very rarely schedule any new projects to start during this time frame, and if a project is near completion, every effort is made to wrap it up before the holidays.

When I arrived at my office on Monday morning following the Thanksgiving break, I was surprised to find a voicemail message from Sally White. Sally and I had been e-mailing back and forth about her team's project to enhance one of our purchasing systems. When we spoke last, Sally was trying to implement some structured project management processes to ensure this effort did not become any larger. I decided to swing by her office after grabbing a cup of coffee.

Sally was in her mid-30s and happily single. She had light brown hair and hazel eyes and was an avid reader. She had three bookcases in her office, and they were all full to the point of overflowing.

"Tom, I have some good news today," Sally began with a smile as I walked into her office. "We were able to formally gain agreement on the business requirements for this work. I think the problems I e-mailed you about regarding scope change are all in the past."

"That's good news," I replied, also with a smile. "As I said in one of my replies, you cannot manage scope effectively if you have not defined the scope to begin with."

We talked some more about the requirements. Sally was able to gain agreement on a minimum set of requirements from the manufacturing client. During the discussions, however, Sally uncovered other features that the client wanted. These were not included in the project for the sake of get-ting the initial work completed and implemented.

"When does it look like you will be completed?" I asked.

"We have some more good news on that front," Sally said excitedly. "We initially told the client it would take an additional six weeks to complete the work. But, when we got into the initial programming, we discovered some of the work was not nearly as complex as we first feared. We have about two weeks less work than we thought."

"Great news!" I agreed. "I'm sure your client will be happy to implement this work earlier."

"Well, that is one option," Sally countered. "However, remember we uncov-ered a number of additional features the client wanted, but did not include in this enhancement. Now that we have some extra time, we can include this additional work as well. I think the client will be very happy when they see the extra features we will be able to implement, and still deliver within the dead-line they have already agreed to."

"Has your client approved the extra features?" I asked.

Sally looked a little puzzled. "Well, we did not ask them officially. We thought it would be a nice surprise if we delivered the extra features. We know they wanted them initially."

On the surface, this sounded great. But, I knew from experience and training this was not the right way to go. Sally was about to get into a case of goldplating.

LESSON 47

DON'T PRACTICE GOLDPLATING—DELIVERING MORE THAN THE CLIENT REQUESTED

In general, project managers should always strive to set expectations care-fully and then to meet those expectations. Setting expectations is one of the reasons we ask the sponsor and key stakeholders to approve the Project Definition and the business requirements. If the project manager can then deliver within those expectations, the project is typically consid-ered a success. However, like Sally, you may also have heard it is good to under-promise and over-deliver. Let's first look at what it means to under-promise, since there is a good way and a bad way to do this.

The project manager has some options when setting expectations. In general, you can estimate work based on one of three scenarios—worst case, most likely, and best case. The worst-case option means you assume everything will go wrong. Work will take longer than you expect, issues will come up, potential risks will occur, etc. If you give your client an estimate based on the worst-case scenario, you are not under-promising. You are sandbagging, which means you are purposely setting very low expectations you know you can exceed. Sandbagging is not good because you are not presenting reasonable and accurate information to the client, and therefore the client does not have the right facts available to make the best business decision.

The best-case scenario is just the opposite. If you present the best case, you are assuming everything will go according to plan and everything will work great the first time. This is also not a good estimate to present to the client, for the same reason that worst-case numbers are not good. The client cannot make the best business decisions if the project estimates are skewed one way or another.

You could present the client three estimates—worst case, best case, and most likely. That would give them valid numbers within the proper context. However, if you are only going to provide one estimate (which is usually the case), you want to provide the estimate that you feel is most likely to occur.

With that in mind, let's look back at Sally's desire to under-promise and over-deliver. She has set reasonable expectations and now is able to exceed those expectations. Won't the client be happy because Sally is able to deliver more than they have requested?

Even though it might appear to be a good thing, this is actually not good practice. The term *goldplating* refers to the act of delivering more than the client has requested. It is wrong for two reasons. First, the primary focus of the project should be to make sure you deliver what the client wants, on time and within budget. By adding additional work, the risk increases that the project will actually miss its deadline. If Sally's misses her deadline date, no one will want to hear that the date was missed because Sally added additional work to the project that the client did not ask for.

Second, Sally is taking it upon herself to make a business decision on what is of most value to the client. There may be some good reasons why the additional features were not included in her initial project scope. They may, in fact, have had marginal value for the client. There may be more value in having the solution implemented two weeks earlier. The point is this is a client decision and not one the IT project manager should make.

The bottom line is you should meet your commitments. It is also a good practice to under-promise and over-deliver. However, the over-deliver part of the equation needs to apply to delivering earlier or for less cost than was anticipated. It should not include delivering more requirements than were asked for. If you can deliver earlier or for less cost, let the client make the decision on what to do with his or her good fortune.

48

Marc Finds the Work Slipping When Everyone Is Responsible

STEP 3 MANAGE THE WORKPLAN

Several people in my section of the office were taking vacation time in December, and I was amazed at how quiet the hallways and corridors were with fewer people around. I could actually hear the Christmas music coming from Leon Hart's office, and he worked about six doors down from me. I decided I would visit some project managers in their offices so I could escape the noise.

My first opportunity to talk to someone came when I met with Marc Reynolds to discuss his project to build a customized time reporting application for all IT contractors. Marc was an older man, probably in his late 50s, and did not ask for help on his projects. In fact, the only reason we were meeting was because his boss had called me and asked me to check in on him. Apparently, Marc's project had encountered some trouble about a month ago, but the team had been able to solve it and get back on schedule—at least up until two weeks ago. Now they were falling behind again.

"We are getting over the hump," Marc said in response to my question about his project status. "But as we are getting to the end of the project, I'm asking the team to do quite a bit of multitasking. As a result, some team members are having difficulty completing their assignments on time."

"It's not uncommon to have a rash of work to complete at the end of the project," I agreed. "This is the time where discipline and time management skills are so valuable. Tell me more about why the work is falling behind. Does everyone know what's expected of them?"

"I sure hope so!" Marc exclaimed. "I've tried to make it simple by dividing the group into two subteams. Each subteam is responsible for about half the remaining work."

"That sounds reasonable," I replied. "What does your team say about missing their deadlines now that the project is so close to completion?"

"That's one of the frustrating side effects of having two subteams. I'm try-ing to give the teams maximum flexibility to complete their assigned work in whatever way makes the most sense. However, since I am assigning work to a team, I don't really know who to hold accountable when deadline dates are missed."

I could start to see a problem. "Marc," I said, "you may have taken the team concept a little too far. Although the work is given to a team, you still need to assign someone to be responsible for each activity. When people are working on multiple activities at the same time, it is especially important to have someone accountable for each activity."

LESSON 48

MAKE SURE ONE PERSON IS RESPONSIBLE FOR EACH ACTIVITY IN THE WORKPLAN

On a perfect team, all members would understand what is expected of them, and the members would all hold themselves accountable for meeting the expectations. There are actually some teams like this. These mature teams are sometimes called *high-performing teams.* Typically, work is assigned to the team and the team figures out how to do it. No project manager or team leader is needed. However, it normally takes several years for teams to reach that high-performing state.

In the real world, almost all teams fall short of this idealistic goal. When normal teams are asked to suddenly take on some of the traits of a high-performing team, they can struggle. Sometimes the struggle can lead them to a higher level of performance more quickly. In most cases, how-ever, a team presented with this situation will descend into confusion and chaos.

People don't always understand what is expected of them when they are left to work without proper guidance. In many cases, they overempha-size certain activities to the detriment of others. If there are problems, no one steps up to deal with them. In the worst case, anarchy breaks out as people thrash around amongst various activities, without the focus needed to complete any of them on time. One of the purposes of having a project manager is to provide that central focus for leading and managing people on the project. On many projects, the project manager is the only person who maintains enough overall perspective to make the right deci-sions in terms of priorities and resource requirements.

Just as a project needs one project manager, so each activity needs to have one person assigned to the responsibility and accountability for completing the work on time. If only one person is assigned to the work, the responsibility naturally falls on him or her. When activities are assigned to multiple members, one person still needs to be responsible for ensuring the work gets done. This one person is responsible for providing status, escalating issues, and making scope change requests, and is accountable when work is not completed on time.

Marc has reorganized his project team into two subteams that he feels reflects the two major components of remaining work. He has restructured the team in a creative attempt to complete the remaining work as efficiently as possible. He feels if each team focuses on one of the two remaining areas of work, they could complete the work much faster.

His idea may be a good one, but there is a problem with one aspect of how the teams were implemented. He has opened the door to a potential loss of focus by not assigning one person to be responsible for each remaining activity. Since each team has a number of activities assigned to it, team members are working on more than one thing. This multitasking has left a vacuum in terms of responsibility. When work is trending late, there is no one with the authority or with the responsibility to prioritize the work to ensure that it is completed as efficiently as is possible. If problems arise, it is not clear who is responsible for resolving them. Each team member is assigned to other activities, so there is a tendency to work where there are no problems, and let the problem areas languish. This would not happen on a mature, high-performing team, but Marc's subteams are not at that level yet.

Marc is not going to develop a high-performing team overnight. So, his short-term solution is to make sure every activity has a responsible person assigned to it. This does not have to be the same person. He can assign each of the members of a subteam to be responsible for specific activities.

In this way, each activity has one person who is responsible for making sure that it is completed on time. If problems arise, each responsible person will have the responsibility for resolving them, or bringing them to Marc's attention. If they are not getting the necessary time from other team members, they can raise a concern to Marc. They have an interest in making sure the activity is completed successfully.

So it is with all workplans. If multiple people are assigned to one activity, the project manager must be clear on who has the overall responsibility for completion.

49

Lauren Needs to Complete a Never-Ending Project

STEP 3 MANAGE THE WORKPLAN

A week before the Christmas holiday, I paid a visit to Lauren Carter, the project manager responsible for moving the old shop floor batch reports to the Web. When I last met with her, she was only a couple weeks away from finishing the project. It had now been six weeks, and she was still four weeks away from finishing. I again took advantage of the opportunity to leave my part of the building, and paid a visit to Lauren in her office. I also liked going to her office because she had a large display of sports memorabilia. She had several basketballs from her high school days, commemorating the records she had broken, but she also had several autographed balls and jerseys. My favorite was a pair of sneakers autographed by Michael Jordan.

"What's going on Lauren?" I asked from outside her office.

"Come on in, Tom. Not much happening here, just trying to get this project finished."

"It seems to be going on much longer than you had anticipated, yet I don't see or hear any indication that you are behind schedule."

"There have been a number of scope changes requiring us to push the end date out," Lauren said. "However, you will be glad to know I am invoking scope change management. Our sponsor approves each change, so we have been getting extra funding and extensions on our deadline."

"That explains why no one is complaining," I noted. "What types of change requests are you receiving?"

"They are mostly for additional features and functions, and small changes to our current deliverables," Lauren said, yawning. "That's one reason why we have been able to accommodate most of them successfully. They don't require a lot of work from our team."

"What does the future look like?" I asked. "Are you going to be able to complete the project by the end of January?"

"It's not clear," Lauren replied a bit apprehensively. "Most of the shop floor supervisors have never had extensive Web experience. Now that they are getting more familiar with the technology, they are finding more and more things they want to incorporate."

"That's not entirely good," I said with some concern. "Projects are temporary endeavors to produce a set of deliverables. They need to end at some point. I'm afraid you may be in a position where your project goes on and on, with minor changes bringing only incremental and marginal business value."

"You are right," Lauren agreed. "In fact, I think the team is starting to lose focus and energy. I have some concerns that we are getting a little sloppy in our testing and we may end up missing something."

"Let's talk with your sponsor about bringing the project to a close," I suggested. "This doesn't mean that your clients will not have the chance to make additional changes. If there is business value in additional modifications, let's consider them to be enhancements after the project goes live."

LESSON 49

FOCUS ON YOUR DEADLINE DATE TO KEEP YOUR PROJECT FROM WANDERING

On most projects, the project sponsor and project team are focused on completing the original work within the agreed budget and deadline. If anything, the team struggles, trying to get all the work done by the deadline. In fact, there are many times when the deadline date may slip a few days so that work is not rushed too fast, causing future implementation problems.

If the project is important enough, you typically don't have time to wander. If you miss a deadline, your manager and client start to get nervous and put pressure on the team to complete the work. The team may start to work overtime or new people may be assigned.

There are also some projects that have no focused end date. They may have an initial target end date, but there is no business driver for the date. It is simply the date on the schedule when the project should be completed. If there is no business driver for the end date, the project deadline is more likely to slip. The deadline date may get pushed out when scope change requests get approved. At other times, the team may not be able to get the work done by the original end date and the deadline gets pushed out.

Whenever the deadline date gets extended, it is important for the project manager to refocus the team on the new date. Having a focused end date gives team members a sense of urgency and purpose and helps them to understand the importance of completing their work on time within the context of getting the entire project done on time.

A problem arises, however, when the deadline date changes repeatedly. This can be caused by teams missing their first target date and then missing their revised target date and so on in what seems to be a never-ending cycle of work. This is a very bad situation from the standpoint of team morale and credibility. That is why it is important to make sure your deadline dates represent your best and most likely estimates. If you miss one deadline date, you don't want to miss a second deadline date because your revised estimates were based on a best-case scenario.

Another reason that deadline dates slip repeatedly is because of an ongoing set of scope changes. These projects also don't have a firm business-driven deadline. The sponsor still wants the work completed, but they are flexible on when it happens.

Lauren's project is a great example of this. Her sponsor is lax, and is approving major and minor scope change requests on an ongoing basis, even at the end of the project. This is not scope creep, since the project manager and sponsor are actively managing and approving the changes. However, her sponsor is also introducing risk. There is a growing risk that striving for the perfect solution will cause the team to get careless and unfocused, which could mean lower quality and more problems down the road. The attitude of the team starts to be that the project will finish when it finishes—whenever that is.

At this point, the best for approach for Lauren is to work with the sponsor to freeze all changes. This allows the team to focus on final testing and implementation. New requirements are still permitted, but the team will place them on a prioritized backlog list. This list will be reviewed after the application goes live and is stable. Changes will then be considered application enhancements. They can be worked on by the support organization, or perhaps by planning a new phase II project. However, this first project needs to be wrapped up before the lack of focus leads to new problems.

50 Heather Finds Her Facts Don't Win Any Points

My last meeting of the year was with Heather Cruise. Heather pulled me aside at the annual Christmas lunch, and asked if she could see me sometime before the break. She and I agreed to talk in a few days, and today was as good a day as any. I agreed to meet at her convenience and we set up a time for the afternoon.

Heather was assigned to a project for the Finance Division when the previous project manager resigned. The project was already experiencing some problems, which was probably a factor in the previous project manager leaving the country. It was a tough spot for Heather, but she had done an admirable job in bringing the project to completion. Although the solution was finally implemented, there was still some question as to whether the project was successful or not. I attended the project conclusion meeting and I could tell it did not go as Heather had expected. She came prepared with a set of metrics to show her team was somewhat successful on the project, but the business client did not accept her metrics at face value.

"Heather, it appears there was a difference of opinion on whether the project was successful or not," I began. "I first wanted to compliment you. You attempted to initiate a fact-based discussion to show the state of the project. Why do you think it didn't work out the way you planned?"

"There was a lot of emotion built up over the course of the project," Heather replied in a serious tone, her eyes widening. "I came into the project late and didn't realize the level of dissatisfaction some of the clients felt with the previous project manager. Since there was so much emotion involved, I tried to bring the discussion around to some fact-based metrics."

"It sounded like the client was challenging the validity of some of your numbers and whether they were relevant," I noted. "For instance, you said the project completed on schedule, but the client said the solution was implemented without adequate testing."

"That may or may not be the case," Heather countered defensively, shaking her head back and forth. "We all agreed we would implement on the revised deadline date and fix any problems on an ongoing basis. Having agreed to that decision, I don't know how they can complain about the project being late."

"Yes, but the client said they were pushed into that decision because they could not afford to miss this monthly financial close cycle," I noted.

Heather was about to respond, but I realized the current line of reasoning was not going anywhere. Nor should it, since it was not the general lesson I was trying to teach.

"Heather, let me stop you for a minute. You have the right idea about the importance of project metrics. If you measure the right characteristics of your project, you will be in a much better position to improve your processes during the project, and have a fact-based discussion about overall project success or failure. But your metrics seemed to be designed to show the project team in a more favorable light. You also missed a very important part of project success metrics—you must gain agreement with your client ahead of time."

LESSON 50

COLLECT METRICS, BUT GAIN AGREEMENT ON THEIR SIGNIFICANCE AHEAD OF TIME

It has been said there are facts, lies, and then there are statistics. Statistics, or metrics, can be gathered on myriad combinations of project team and deliverable characteristics. For instance, you can collect metrics on the height of team members, the number of reporting errors, the daily high temperature in Dickens, and the cost of a project. Although there are dozens (or hundreds) of metrics you can gather, some of them are obviously more relevant and significant to the project than others.

One of the purposes of metrics is to objectively determine how successful a project was. However, the project manager cannot pick an arbitrary set of metrics to indicate success. It is the client, and specifically the sponsor, who ultimately determines project success. You could just ask the sponsor if the project was a success or not. However, gathering metrics gives you a more objective way to measure success rather than just relying on the perception (or the whim) of the sponsor.

One of the purposes of gaining agreement on the initial Project Definition is that it provides a set of deliverables upon which success or failure can be measured. The project manager should be aware of these when gathering metrics during the project. Delivering the agreed upon deliverables could be the starting point for a set of project success metrics.

Heather understood that metrics were important to try to show project success. She realized that without more facts, the client was going to conclude the project was a disaster. However, she failed to do two important things. First, she failed to get an agreement with the sponsor on the significance and the interpretation of the metrics she chose. Second, she did not make sure the metrics were balanced and broad enough to represent the reality of the project experience. Since there was a disagreement on the metrics gathered and what they meant, Heather was challenged right away.

Heather's business client was not happy with the way the project was run and was not happy with the system that was implemented. So, not surprisingly, they didn't agree with metrics saying the project was a success or a partial success. Heather's metrics seemed to be a narrow set attempting to show the results in as favorable a light as possible.

Heather would have been better off proposing a wider range of metrics to her client. These would have included

- Actual costs expended compared to the budget
- Actual delivery date compared to the original deadline
- Quantitative metrics describing the solution's performance, including response time and defects
- Qualitative metrics describing client satisfaction with the solution, including ease of use, look and feel, etc.
- Survey feedback describing the client's satisfaction with how the project team performed, including how quickly the team responded to problems, how well they communicated, how well they partnered, etc.

Heather should have made sure there was an agreement with the sponsor on the metrics to collect and how to interpret the results. Normally this is done at the beginning of the project. However, since Heather came to the project late, she should have gained agreement when she first came on board. Then her team could have focused on the proper success factors, and, when the project ended, she could have collected the metrics and have the fact-based discussion she was hoping for. Since she would need to take client satisfaction into account, the final results were still not going to be pretty. However, a good set of metrics does give everyone the right facts with which to have a discussion about what went right and what could be improved. If you have an unapproved, arbitrary, and skewed set of metrics, you are not going to get anywhere in a discussion.

YEAR-END RECAP

I have enjoyed my job over the past year, and I hope I was able to provide value to the project managers in the IT Division. The preceding stories represent only a fraction of the meetings and coaching sessions I participated in during the year. I have tried to pick out stories that highlight the most valuable project management lessons. Of course, there are many others as well.

The year had not only been fun, but it had been professionally rewarding for two reasons. First, I had been able to see project managers learn and grow. My work allowed me to meet all sorts of project managers. Many were already skilled in the project management discipline, while others had never before received formal training or coaching, and didn't really know what it meant to manage a project. These were people like Jerry Ackerman.

Of course, the majority of project managers were in between. People like Lindsay, Sean, and Ashley. They came from various organizations, but all had some project management skills—even a little training. However, they managed projects by being well organized, with a sense for how to organize and manage the work, rather than by utilizing specific project management methodologies.

Second, my work this year has set the stage for the real project management deployment initiative scheduled to begin next year. Our CIO feels there is much more value to be gained by managing projects more efficiently and consistently. I don't think we are doing a bad job today of managing projects. In fact, probably the majority of our projects have been completed more or less within expectations. However, can those expectations be raised? Probably so.

The way to implement project management processes in a large organization is through a focused Project Management Office (PMO). Mega Manufacturing realized this as well. Our CIO wanted to start a major initiative this year to build a PMO and then use the PMO to deploy a common set of project management processes, templates, best practices, etc., across the organization. However, budget tightening and a number of other business initiatives forced this broader initiative to be postponed for a year.

My position was funded as a temporary measure to start to prepare project managers for this larger initiative. My role as a project management advisor is one part of this broader PMO-focused project. However, there is much more. We need to build and staff a PMO, and then use the

PMO to acquire/build a common project management methodology, provide a common level of training, and build a set of common project management templates. We then need to embark down the long road of ensuring the new processes stick. This type of effort is a culture change initiative. It forces changes in how people do their jobs. The initiative requires staying power and strong executive sponsorship.

The CIO's plan for establishing the Project Management Office has been approved. The project is being funded as a three-year initiative, after which the PMO will move from deployment mode to the long-term support and care of the project management process. It promises to be challenging—culture change always is. However, I hope the work I have done this year has set the stage for this broader initiative in the years ahead. If we are successful, a new project driven culture will emerge, allowing all project managers to successfully deliver projects faster, with higher quality, and at less cost than we do today.

Wish us luck in this initiative (perhaps this initiative would make for a good book in the future).

—

Appendix

Project Management Templates

This book contains a bonus CD-ROM with 25 project management templates, described in the following table, that cover various project management steps from the TenStep Project Management Process (http://www.tenstep.com). These are templates you can use on your project. They can be utilized as is, or modified to meet the particular needs of your organization or your project.

Essential Project Management Templates

Project Management Step	Template	Description
Step 1 Define the Work	Project Definition	(Large projects) The full Project Definition defines large work efforts. This template is used to ensure the work is defined adequately and is properly approved. This document also serves to set expectations with the business client regarding the work requested. The sections in the document include Project Executive Summary, Project Overview, Project Objectives, Project Scope, Project Estimated Effort/Cost/Duration, Project Assumptions, Project Risks, Project Approach, Project Organization, Project Approvals.
	Abbreviated Project Definition	(Medium-sized projects) The Abbreviated Project Definition defines medium-sized work efforts. This template is used to ensure the work is defined at the appropriate level and is properly approved before work begins. The definition process is not as extensive as the full Project Definition, given the work effort is not nearly as large. This document also serves to set expectations with the business client regarding the work requested. The sections in the document include Project Overview, Scope, Project Estimated Effort/Cost/Duration, Project Assumptions, Project Risks, Project Approvals.

Essential Project Management Templates *(continued)*

Project Management Step	Template	Description
	Service Request	(Small projects) The Service Request defines small work efforts. This template is used to ensure the work is defined adequately and properly approved. Because the work effort is small, the level of definition required is much less rigorous than what is specified in the Abbreviated Project Definition (medium-sized projects) or a full Project Definition (large projects). Although the information required on the Service Request is not extensive, the document still serves to set expectations with the business client regarding the work requested.
	Project Management Procedures	The Project Management Procedures describe how the project will be managed, and are an effective way to communicate the processes to the project team, customers, and stakeholders. They should be customized as appropriate for your project, your team, and your organization. In most cases, the processes should be simplified for smaller projects.
Step 3 Manage the Workplan	Action Item Log	The Action Item Log contains a summary of all the action items that come up during the life of the project. Action items typically arise as follow-up work from meetings or from activities needing more work. This log is used to keep track of the action items, the person responsible, and the deadline date. An alternative to this Action Item Log is to add all action items as activities to the project workplan.
Step 4 Manage Issues	Issues Log	The Issues Log contains a summary of all open and closed issues. Use it to view open issues and make sure a resolution is proceeding. The log should contain enough information to ensure issues are not overlooked, but should not be so detailed that scanning becomes difficult.
	Issue Submission Form	Larger projects need more rigor and structure in how issues are raised and managed. The Issue Submission Form is used to capture, screen, prioritize, and evaluate issues. Each form should describe one specific issue.

Essential Project Management Templates *(continued)*

Project Management Step	Template	Description
Step 5 Manage Scope	Scope Change Log	The Scope Change Log contains a summary of all pending, open, and closed scope change requests. Use it to track all scope change requests, and to ensure the scope change resolution process is proceeding. The log should contain enough information to ensure scope changes are not overlooked, but should not be so detailed that scanning them becomes difficult.
	Scope Change Request Form	Larger projects need more rigor and structure in how they raise and manage scope change requests. The Scope Change Request Form is used to capture, assign, prioritize, and evaluate scope changes. Each form should describe one specific scope change request.
Step 6 Manage Communication	Individual Status Report	The Individual Status Report is used by project team members to communicate regularly and formally with their project managers, informing them of the current status of the project and managing future expectations. The project manager should be talking to the team on an ongoing basis, but this report allows for a formal, documented communication of progress.
	Project Status Report	Project managers should communicate regularly to stakeholders, informing them of the current status of the project and managing future expectations. The Project Status Report, along with status meetings and other proactive communication, should ensure there are no surprises.
	Project Status Report (Summary)	Project managers should communicate regularly to stakeholders, informing them of the current status of the project and managing future expectations. This Project Status Report is designed to provide a higher-level summary of a number of projects. This might be a format more appropriate for a roll-up report sent to the CIO.

Essential Project Management Templates *(continued)*

Project Management Step	Template	Description
	Communication Plan	Proactive communication is important on all projects. However, communication gets much more complex the larger a project gets and the more people involved. Larger projects require planned communication, taking into account the particular needs of the people involved. The Communication Plan allows you to plan for how to communicate most efficiently and effectively to the various constituents.
	Milestone Summary Report	The Milestone Summary Report is completed at the end of every major milestone. This report provides an opportunity to share the progress of the project and validate everything is in position to continue. The format of the report is more like a memo, since the target audience is management stakeholders.
	Project Kickoff Meeting Agenda	This template shows the agenda for a kickoff meeting. A kickoff meeting is used to gather all the stakeholders together and to formally announce the project has started.
Step 7 Manage Risk	Inherent Project Risk Factors Checklist	This template is used to determine whether there are inherent risks on your project, based on its general characteristics. For instance, a project estimated to take 10,000 effort hours is inherently more risky than one that takes 1,000 effort hours. The results should be used as guidelines, since other factors may lower or raise the risk level. For instance, the higher risk inherent in a larger project may be reduced with an experienced project manager.
Step 8 Manage Documents	Version Tracking Page	This template is used to keep track of important documents that will be updated a number of times during its lifetime. The original document creation is called version 1.0. After that, subsequent updates can be 2.0, 3.0, etc. Incremental versions can be 1.1, 1.2, 1.3, etc. When you want to use version control on a document, insert this page toward the beginning of the document (say, after the cover page), or at the very end.

Essential Project Management Templates *(continued)*

Project Management Step	Template	Description
Step 9 Manage Quality	Quality Plan	The Quality Plan is done during the definition step to ensure major deliverables are completed with an acceptable level of quality. There are three sections: Completeness and Correctness Criteria (see the next entry), Quality Assurance Activities, and Quality Control Activities.
	Completeness and Correctness Criteria	The purpose of the Completeness and Correctness template is to work with the customer up front to define when a deliverable is complete and correct. If you define the criteria and expectations up front, you will be better able to meet the customer's expectations. In other words, there should be no surprises. This document can be created as a stand-alone deliverable, or this information can be included in the Quality Plan (see the preceding entry).
	Project Assessment Summary	The purpose of this template is to summarize how a project is performing. It represents a quick audit that provides a snapshot of how well a project is being managed. Project managers can use this form to assess their own project performance. However, it is more likely a third party will be asked to do the assessment. The assessment looks at where the project is in its life cycle, and whether the project manager is successfully managing scope, risk, issues, communication, etc.
	End-of-Project Assessment	At the end of every project, the team should meet with the key customers and stakeholders. The objective of the meeting is to gain a consensus on what went right and wrong, so the good things are done again and the wrong things are avoided. After the meeting, this information should be documented and circulated so others have an opportunity to learn from the experience. If the organization captures this learning, it should be submitted to the appropriate repository.

Essential Project Management Templates *(continued)*

Project Management Step	Template	Description
	Quality Assurance Checklist for Outsourced Projects	If you outsource a project to a third-party company, you also outsource the day-to-day project management responsibilities. However, your company still needs to have a level of involvement to validate the outsourcer will deliver within your expectations. This Quality Assurance Checklist for Outsourced Projects contains criteria necessary to verify the up-front agreements include the information necessary to subsequently manage the relationship. It also verifies the project is proceeding on track and that you know about any deviations from plan, and the project concludes as you expect based on the Project Definition and contract.
Step 10 Manage Metrics	Project Scorecard	Large projects should be capturing metrics to provide information on the quality of the deliverables and the processes used to create the deliverables. The Project Scorecard template takes you though a process of identifying critical success factors, and determining a good set of balanced metrics that would indicate whether your project was successful.
	Customer Satisfaction Survey	Gathering client satisfaction metrics is important because it allows you to see how you are performing against the expectations of your customers. One way to gather this information is with customer satisfaction surveys. Surveys are by their nature qualitative, that is, they reflect the opinion of the person being surveyed. However, for many types of metrics, a qualitative survey question can be asked as a substitute for the quantitative metric.
	End-of-Project Metrics Worksheet	The purpose of the End of Project Metrics Worksheet is to capture a consistent set of metrics so your organization can see the trends for delivering projects over a period of time. The metrics show how well project teams are meeting their commitments in terms of quality, cost, and cycle time. As more and more projects report the metrics, a baseline will be established to compare to over time.

Glossary

Activity

For the purposes of the TenStep Project Management Process, an activity is the smallest unit of work identified in the project workplan (in other methodologies, an activity may be broken down even further into tasks).

Assumption

There may be external circumstances or events that must occur for the project to be successful. If you believe these external events are likely to happen, then you have an assumption (contrast with the definition of a risk). If an event is within the control of the project team, such as having testing completed by a certain date, then it is not an assumption. If an event has a 100 percent chance of occurring, then it not an assumption, since there is no "likelihood" or risk involved (it is just a fact). Examples of assumptions might be "Budgets and resources will be available when needed," or "The new software release will be available for use by the time the construct phase begins."

Client

The persons or groups benefiting directly from a project or service. The people for whom a project is undertaken (indirect beneficiaries are probably stakeholders). If the persons or groups are internal, TenStep refers to them as *clients*. If they are external, TenStep refers to them as *customers*.

Critical path

The sequence of activities that must be completed on schedule for the entire project to be completed on schedule. This is the longest duration path through the workplan. If an activity on the critical path is delayed by one day, the entire project will be delayed by one day (unless another activity on the critical path can be accelerated by one day).

Customer

The persons or groups benefiting directly from a project or service. The people for whom a project is undertaken (indirect beneficiaries are probably stakeholders). If the persons or groups are internal, TenStep refers to them as *clients*. If they are external, TenStep refers to them as *customers*.

Deliverable

A deliverable is any tangible outcome produced by the project. These can be documents, plans, computer systems, buildings, aircraft, etc. Internal deliverables are produced as a consequence of executing the project, and are usually only needed by the project team. External deliverables are created for customers and stakeholders.

Functional manager

The functional manager is the person project managers report to within their functional organization. Typically, they do the performance review. Project managers may also be functional managers, but they do not have to be. If the project manager is different from the functional manager, then the organization is probably utilizing matrix management.

Issue

An issue is a major problem that will impede the progress of the project and cannot be resolved by the project manager and project team without outside help.

Life cycle

The process used to build and support the project deliverables (since a project has a start date and end date, the long-term support of a solution is usually performed after the project is completed). For software development, the entire life cycle might consist of planning, analysis, design, construct/test, implementation, and support.

Milestone

A milestone is a scheduled event signifying the completion of a major deliverable or a set of related deliverables. A milestone has zero duration and no effort—there is no work associated with a milestone. It is a flag in the workplan to signify some other work has completed. Usually a milestone is used as a project checkpoint to validate how the project is progressing and revalidate work. Milestones are also used as high-level snapshots for management to validate the progress of the project. In many cases there is a decision to be made at a milestone. However, the milestone is not usually based on the calendar. It is usually based on the completion of one or more deliverables.

Objective

A concrete statement describing what the project is trying to achieve. The objective should be written at a low level so it can be evaluated at the conclusion of a project to determine whether it was achieved or not. A well-worded objective will be *S*pecific, *M*easurable, *A*ttainable/Achievable, *R*ealistic, and *T*imebound (SMART).

Program

A program is the umbrella structure established to manage a series of related projects. The program does not produce any project deliverables. The project teams produce them all. The purpose of the program is to provide overall direction and guidance, make sure the related projects are communicating effectively, provide a central point of contact and focus for the customer and the project teams, and determine how individual projects should be defined to ensure all the work gets completed successfully.

Program manager

The person with authority to manage a program. (Note: This is a role. The program manager may also be responsible for one or more of the projects within the program. He or she would be project manager on those projects as well as overall program manager.) The program manager leads the overall planning and management of the program. All project managers within the program report to the program manager.

Project

A structure to complete a specifically defined deliverable or set of deliverables. A project has a specific begin date and end date, specific objectives, and specific resources assigned to perform the work. A project manager has overall responsibility and authority over a project. When the objectives are met, the project is considered complete.

Project manager

The person with authority to manage a project. This includes leading the planning and the development of all project deliverables. The project manager is responsible for managing the budget, workplan, and all project management procedures (scope management, issues management, risk management, etc.).

Project phase

A logical grouping of work on a project. A phase also represents the completion of a major deliverable or set of related deliverables. On an IS development project, logical phases might be planning, analysis, design, construct (including testing), and implementation.

Project team

The project team consists of the full-time and part-time resources assigned to work on the deliverables of the project, which will help achieve the project objectives. They are responsible for understanding the work to be completed; planning out the assigned activities in more detail if needed; completing assigned work within the budget, timeline, and quality expectations; informing the project manager of issues, scope changes, risk, and quality concerns; proactively communicating status; and managing expectations.

The project team can consist of human resources within one functional organization, or it can consist of members from many different functional organizations. A cross-functional team has members from multiple organizations. Having a cross-functional team is usually a sign your organization is utilizing matrix management.

Risk

There may be external circumstances or events that *cannot* occur for the project to be successful. If you believe such an event is likely to happen, then it would be a risk (contrast with the definition of an assumption). Identifying something as a risk increases its visibility, and allows a proactive risk management plan to be put into place. If an event is within the control of the project team, such as having testing complete by a certain date, then it is not a risk. If an event has a 100 percent chance of occurring, then it not a risk, since there is no "likelihood" or risk involved (it is just a fact). Examples of risks might be "Reorganization may result in key people being reassigned," or "The new hardware may not be able to handle the expected sales volume."

Scope

Scope describes the boundaries of the project. It defines what the project will and will not deliver. For larger projects, it can include the organizations affected, the transactions affected, the data types included, etc.

Sponsor (executive sponsor and project sponsor)

The person with ultimate authority over the project. The executive sponsor provides project funding, resolves issues and scope changes, approves major deliverables, and provides high-level direction. This person also champions the project within his or her organization. Depending on the project, and the organizational level of the executive sponsor, he or she may delegate day-to-day tactical management to a project sponsor. If assigned, the project sponsor represents the executive sponsor on a day-to-day basis, and makes most of the decisions requiring sponsor approval. If the decision is large enough, the project sponsor will take it to the executive sponsor.

Stakeholder

Specific persons or groups who have a stake in the outcome of the project. Normally stakeholders are from within the company, and could include internal customers, management, employees, administrators, etc. A project may also have external stakeholders, including suppliers, investors, community groups, and government organizations.

Standard

A *required* approach for conducting an activity or task, utilizing a product, etc. Many times a standard is a best practice that must be followed to have a better chance of overall success.

Steering committee

A group of high-level stakeholders who are responsible for providing guidance on overall strategic direction. They do not take the place of a sponsor, but help to spread the strategic input and buy-in to a larger portion of the organization. The steering committee is usually made up of organizational peers, and is a combination of direct customers and indirect stakeholders.

Apress®

LICENSE AGREEMENT (SINGLE-USER PRODUCTS)

THIS IS A LEGAL AGREEMENT BETWEEN YOU, THE END USER, AND APRESS. BY OPENING THE SEALED DISK PACKAGE, YOU ARE AGREEING TO BE BOUND BY THE TERMS OF THIS AGREEMENT. IF YOU DO NOT AGREE TO THE TERMS OF THIS AGREEMENT, PROMPTLY RETURN THE UNOPENED DISK PACKAGE AND THE ACCOMPANYING ITEMS (INCLUDING WRITTEN MATERIALS AND BINDERS AND OTHER CONTAINERS) TO THE PLACE YOU OBTAINED THEM FOR A FULL REFUND.

APRESS SOFTWARE LICENSE

1. GRANT OF LICENSE. Apress grants you the right to use one copy of this enclosed Apress software program (the "SOFTWARE") on a single terminal connected to a single computer (e.g., with a single CPU). You may not network the SOFTWARE or otherwise use it on more than one computer or computer terminal at the same time.

2. COPYRIGHT. The SOFTWARE copyright is owned by Apress and is protected by United States copyright laws and international treaty provisions. Therefore, you must treat the SOFTWARE like any other copyrighted material (e.g., a book or musical recording) except that you may either (a) make one copy of the SOFTWARE solely for backup or archival purposes, or (b) transfer the SOFTWARE to a single hard disk, provided you keep the original solely for backup or archival purposes. You may not copy the written material accompanying the SOFTWARE.

3. OTHER RESTRICTIONS. You may not rent or lease the SOFTWARE, but you may transfer the SOFTWARE and accompanying written materials on a permanent basis provided you retain no copies and the recipient agrees to the terms of this Agreement. You may not reverse engineer, decompile, or disassemble the SOFTWARE. If SOFTWARE is an update, any transfer must include the update and all prior versions.

4. By breaking the seal on the disc package, you agree to the terms and conditions printed in the Apress License Agreement. If you do not agree with the terms, simply return this book with the still-sealed CD package to the place of purchase for a refund.

DISCLAIMER OF WARRANTY

NO WARRANTIES. Apress disclaims all warranties, either express or implied, including, but not limited to, implied warranties of merchantability and fitness for a particular purpose, with respect to the SOFTWARE and the accompanying written materials. The software and any related documentation is provided "as is." You may have other rights, which vary from state to state.

NO LIABILITIES FOR CONSEQUENTIAL DAMAGES. In no event shall be liable for any damages whatsoever (including, without limitation, damages from loss of business profits, business interruption, loss of business information, or other pecuniary loss) arising out of the use or inability to use this Apress product, even if Apress has been advised of the possibility of such damages. Because some states do not allow the exclusion or limitation of liability for consequential or incidental damages, the above limitation may not apply to you.

U.S. GOVERNMENT RESTRICTED RIGHTS

The SOFTWARE and documentation are provided with RESTRICTED RIGHTS. Use, duplication, or disclosure by the Government is subject to restriction as set forth in subparagraph (c) (1) (ii) of The Rights in Technical Data and Computer Software clause at 52.227-7013. Contractor/manufacturer is Apress, 2560 Ninth Street, Suite 219, Berkeley, California, 94710.

This Agreement is governed by the laws of the State of California.

Should you have any questions concerning this Agreement, or if you wish to contact Apress for any reason, please write to Apress, 2560 Ninth Street, Suite 219, Berkeley, California, 94710.